BANKERS WHO SELL
IMPROVING SELLING
EFFECTIVENESS IN BANKING

BANKERS WHO SELL
IMPROVING SELLING
EFFECTIVENESS IN BANKING

Leonard L. Berry
Charles M. Futrell
Michael R. Bowers

BANK MARKETING ASSOCIATION
Chicago, IL 60606

An affiliate of
**American Bankers
Association**

DOW JONES-IRWIN
Homewood, Illinois   60430

The opinions expressed in this publication are those of
the authors and not necessarily those of BMA, its officers,
or its directors.

ISBN 0-87094-629-3

Library of Congress Catalog Card No. 84–73198

Printed in the United States of America

2 3 4 5 6 7 8 9 0 BC 2 1 0 9 8 7 6 5

Preface

Improving the selling effectiveness of bankers has become one of the banking industry's hottest topics. Recognition is taking hold in the industry that bankers must sell—that they must go after the business, not just wait for it. Deregulation, intense competition, profit pressures, and a changing product line, among other influences, demand no less. Yet, recognizing the need to sell is not enough. Recognition must translate into action—effective action, smart action—for banks to install the sales programs they need to install.

Clearly, the banking industry is struggling in making the transition to selling effectiveness. We know this from the many conversations we have had with bank executives over the past several years concerning problems they were experiencing in developing sales programs in their banks. We know this from the types of questions we are asked by bankers attending our sales workshops. We know this from the research study we report on in this book.

The mid-80s is an "in-between" period for the banking industry. Many bank CEOs, presidents, senior line officers, and marketing directors want their bankers to be more than "order-takers." But they haven't yet accomplished this transformation in most cases. It is turning out to be a tough job. There are traditions to be undone. Culture to be changed. New mind-sets to be developed. Fears and prejudices concerning selling to be overcome. New systems and procedures to be established. And, of course, money to be spent. No, make that money to be *invested*. Real money, not pin money.

Bank marketing directors often complain that top management wants a selling program but that when push comes to shove, management is unwilling to set the priorities and invest the dollars required to get the job done. Sometimes these complaints are justified. On other occasions, however, we sense the real problem is not that top-level managers are unwilling to take the necessary steps but, rather, that they are unsure of what steps to take. They are asked to invest in a piece of a sales program—a new compensation system, for example—but they are not confident that this by itself will prove successful. They know that an integrated program is needed, but they don't know what the program should entail. So they resist "pieces" of the puzzle because they do not know what the pieces will be a part of and where they will lead.

We have spent the past several years working on the question of the bank sales puzzle. The pieces of the puzzle. How they fit together. What the puzzle looks like when completed. This book is the culmination of that work; we present our version of the bank sales puzzle using a framework we call "The Sales Loop Model." The Sales Loop Model is the result of our research with 10 banks throughout the United States that have achieved considerable success in building sales programs. Much of the book concerns what we learned from these 10 banks, although we do incorporate into the book many of our own (pre-research) ideas about selling and marketing in banking, as well as key concepts and findings from the existing literature. Plus, we present the findings from the first phase of our research—a national study of the state of selling in 714 banks—in Chapter 2. But the guts of the book are what we learned from these 10 banks.

One might legitimately ask if 10 banks are enough to write a book about. The answer is "yes," if they are the right banks. Actually, in this research we found so much that was common in the approaches the banks were following that our results probably wouldn't have been materially different had we studied six or seven of the banks, rather than all 10. The 10 sample banks differed in the maturity of their sales programs. Some had well-oiled, highly successful programs. Others were still in the process of fitting all the puzzle pieces together.

The opportunity to compare sales programs having all of the puzzle pieces in place with sales programs missing one or two of the pieces proved invaluable to us. It was invaluable because it reinforced the critical importance of *completing* the puzzle. Comparing, for example, a bank that handles every step in building a sales program well with a bank that handles every step, except reward systems, well makes one a true believer in reward systems.

We do not answer every conceivable question about developing a sales program in this book. It is a complex subject, and we intend to continue our own development and learning in this area. This is not our last book on the subject. What we intend with this book is to provide a framework for thinking about sales program development in a bank. We have also tried to offer ideas, concepts, and guidelines for implementing the framework. We are confident the book will prove worthwhile to readers from small banks as well as large ones, to readers interested in commercial market selling as well as those interested in retail market selling, and to readers needing to develop a sales program from scratch as well as those needing to improve an existing program.

The book is not a panacea. We do not pretend that what we say banks should do to develop or improve a sales program is easy to do. We have attempted to write a book that is honest, straightforward, readable, and practical. Most of all, we have tried to write a book that will be *genuinely helpful* to those faced with the task of building—or rescuing—a sales program.

The Bank Marketing Association cooperated in the first phase of the research reported in this book and funded the second phase. We deeply appreciate the fine support and assistance we have received from Charles Bartling, Ray Cheseldine, Barbara Ross, Pat Russell, and Janis White, all members of the BMA staff. We also wish to acknowledge, with special thanks, the efforts of Dennis Hillen of BMA, who has been involved in this project from its inception and has contributed to it in countless ways. We also wish to thank Beverly Williams, who typed the manuscript.

The research with the 10 banks obviously could not have been completed without the cooperation of these banks. We are indebted to the managements of these banks for believing in the worthwhileness of this research, to the 143 bankers from these banks who consented to be interviewed, and to the individuals at each of the banks who helped coordinate our visits. These latter individuals were extremely helpful to us, and they occupy a special place in our thoughts as we write these words. They are listed below in alphabetical order:

J. R. Daniel, Friendly National Bank
Joanie Hartman, Landmark Bank of Orlando

Donald MacKay, Louisiana National Bank
Steven Menge, Fleet National Bank
Walt Patterson, Worthen Bank & Trust Company
Alex Romero, Sunwest Bank of Albuquerque
Richard Snelsire, Wachovia Bank and Trust Company
Jean Stewart, Security Pacific National Bank
Edward Tucker, C & S National Bank of South Carolina
Lou Ann Williams, Wells Fargo Bank

To all of the above-mentioned bankers, to the bankers who gave us their time and their thoughts in the interviews, and to our friends at the Bank Marketing Association, we dedicate this book. And to you, the reader, we say welcome to a journey through the bank sales puzzle.

Leonard L. Berry
Charles M. Futrell
Michael R. Bowers

Contents

Part One

THE
SELLING
ERA

Selling
Is the Future

> "it is important in a deregulated world that management thinking adapts to the new order of things. I can tell you from first-hand experience that there is a strong compulsion to look back longingly on the orderly and stable conditions of the past. But I can also tell you from firsthand experience that events will not wait for you. As complex and chaotic as the new environment may be, it is the only environment that counts. . . ."
>
> *Donald J. Carty, senior vice president/controller, American Airlines, "Marketing in a Deregulated Environment,"* American Banker, *June 28, 1984, p. 8.*

Most banks in America are struggling to become proficient in personal selling. More and more senior bank executives recognize the importance of selling to their institutions, but are finding that getting it done is quite another matter. Developing an ongoing, professional, aggressive sales program—it turns out—is not something easily or quickly accomplished.

Ironically, the origins of the bank marketing field as we know it today were promotion-based. The term *marketing,* used in banking to some extent in the Fifties and routinely in the Sixties, actually referred to the promotional function. Burnishing the bank's image as a "friendly" institution. Running newspaper ads for checking and savings accounts. Conducting giveaways to attract crowds to new branch openings. This was marketing in the early days (Donnelly and Berry, 1981). It was salesmanship in the fancy dress of marketing (Royal Bank Letter, 1983). But it was salesmanship through the media rather than through people. Bank employees were order-takers. Their job was to fulfill the requests that advertising and public relations and promotions encouraged. It was ads that sold, not people.

WHY SELLING IS SO HARD

The nature of banking (borrowing money from one party and lending it to another), its mystique (working in a bank is not like working in a hardware store), and its restricted competitive past (banks basically competing with other banks within clearly defined boundaries) all help to explain the difficulties the industry is now encountering in making the transition from media-based to personal selling-based marketing.

The fact is banks have not *had* to sell until very recently. Indeed, it was often the customer who had to "sell" the banker rather than the other way around.

Today, America's banks employ many people who never before have held a position in which they were asked to sell. Banks did not seek out sales-minded people in their hiring, and sales-minded people did not seek out banks in their job searches. For some, one of banking's attractions was the absence of a selling role. In contrast, those who entered the insurance or securities brokerage business expected to have to sell.

That many in banking today are uncomfortable with the idea of being a salesperson is understandable. People without professional selling experience often think of selling in terms of smooth-talking hustlers who pressure customers into buying products they really don't want to buy. And banking over the years has not attracted the kind of people who see themselves doing this!

Selling also raises self-doubts: "Can I sell?" "Where will I find customers?" "Do I have the background knowledge to answer the tough questions?" "How will I know what to do?" "Will I fall flat on my face?" Selling—a naked activity—can be scary. One either makes the sale or doesn't. Selling performance is visible; selling performance is *measurable!*

Richard Kendall (1984) points out several differences between what he refers to as "mainline banking" and selling:

1. *In mainline banking activities—credit decisions, working past-due accounts, data processing—results flow directly from efforts.* Making a sale, on the other hand, may not occur until the third or fourth call on a prospect; it even may not occur at all. In selling, the relationship between efforts and results is less immediate and less direct.

2. *Mainline banking is reactive.* The bank opens its doors, customers come through them with problems or needs, and the bank acts. The customer assumes the initiative. In selling, however, it is the banker who must assume the initiative—to solve the customer's problem (which may be different from what the customer thinks it is), to cross-sell, to target accounts, to seek out prospects.

Developing an effective selling program on an ongoing basis presents a formidable task. People are the medium of information transfer, problem solving, and persuasion. People are the sellers. Not machines. Not advertisements. Accordingly, all of the challenges normally associated with managing people—selection, motivation, training, supervision, and so forth—come into play when developing a sales program. That personnel are perhaps being asked to do something they have never done before—and do not want to do—makes the challenge all the more imposing.

WHY SELLING IS SO IMPORTANT

Why must banks tackle—and win—the selling challenge? The answer lies in a shifting product line and shifting bank objectives. Financial services are becoming more complex. And there are more of them from which to choose. Banks can market checking or savings accounts without salespeople. Well-executed advertising is sufficient to communicate the service features and benefits of these accounts. Not so with cash management accounts, retirement accounts, variable-rate loans, financial planning services, investment management services, personal and corporate trust services, insurance, commercial credit services. Marketing complex services requires addressing the customer's confusion, answering questions, discussing alternative courses of action; it requires the *interactive dialogue* that only personal selling provides. The more complex the service line, the more "teaching" banks must do. Effective advertising can build awareness and interest for complex services; it can make the selling task far easier. But obtaining the conviction to buy generally requires a salesperson.

For complex products, advertising tends to be more effective in the earlier stages of the buying process and personal selling more effective in the later, decision-making stages. Advertising and selling are complementary rather than interchangeable; the promotional challenge is to use both to best advantage—and that calls for *coordination*. Non-personal promotion still has important roles to play in bank marketing, but it can no longer do the whole job.

Banking's new objective of relationship banking presents another powerful argument in favor of building a personal selling program. Relationship banking concerns satisfying customers' total financial services needs rather than bits and pieces. It is fundamentally different from "order-taking" banking. In order-taking banking, the emphasis is on the moment, on the immediate situation. A prospect enters the banking facility, requests a service, and the order is "filled." In relationship banking, the emphasis is on establishing long-term multiple-service relationships—on turning customers into clients.

Achieving client relationships requires the presence of a banker who will become familiar with the client's needs, take a genuine interest in the client's welfare, help assemble just the right "package" of financial services, and be available *after* the sale, not just before the sale. True relationship banking requires *high-touch* promotion; personal selling is high-touch promotion. In relationship banking, the prospective client "buys" a banker, not just bank services.

The new realities for banking—intense competition from all sides, deregulation, narrow lending spreads, electronic service delivery technologies, savers transformed into investors—present new realities for bank marketing. Everyone—or so it seems—is getting into the financial services business. Insurance companies, retail chains, credit card firms, securities brokers, thrift institutions, and others are all after banks' best customers. Deregulation offers banks fresh opportunities to attract new business . . . and to lose the business they already have.

Bankers can no longer afford to sit back, wait for customers to appear, and "take orders" in today's and tomorrow's marketplace. They must assume the initiative, identify prospects, uncover needs, and then satisfy these needs. Order-taking banking is the past; professional selling is the future!

THE STUDY

To learn as much as we possibly could about selling in banking—the state of the art, the common problems banks are facing in implementing sales programs, the vital success factors in building a sales program—we embarked on a multi-year, two-phase study of personal selling in banking. Our ultimate objective was to learn what banks need to do to make the transition to selling effectiveness. This book presents the findings, conclusions, and implications of that research.

Phase I of the research was a national survey of bank marketing officers concerning the state of selling in their banks. What was being done in the bank to support a sales program? What were the problems? What were the priorities? We wanted to know where the banking industry was with selling before charting where it needed to go.

Phase II of the research involved an in-depth study of 10 banks in the United States that have made considerable progress in developing a sales program. We visited each of the banks and interviewed senior managers, marketing department personnel, supervisors, and contact personnel having sales responsibilities. Would banks with successful sales programs have certain "sales success factors" in common? If so, what were they? And what guidelines and suggestions could be offered to banks wishing to emulate these success factors?

The focus of this book is the result of the Phase II research. We attempt to offer a blueprint for action to bank executives who want to develop a sales program from scratch or to improve the one they already have. Our findings apply to both retail (consumer) selling and wholesale (institutional) selling. We studied both and became convinced that the essential steps in building a sales program are universal.

Chapter 2 highlights our Phase I findings for readers who have not read the journal articles reporting them or who wish to review these findings again. Chapter 3 presents the methodology used in Phase II and introduces a framework to be used throughout the book: the *Sales Loop Model*. Chapters 4 through 12 present the elements of the Sales Loop Model. Chapter 13, the last chapter, summarizes the central themes of the book and offers a series of final thoughts and ideas on successfully implementing a sales program.

The reader will gain more from the book if the final chapter is the last chapter read. We take a step-by-step, building-block approach in this book and recommend that the chapters be read in sequence.

CONCLUSION

Banks in the United States have not really had to sell until recently. An aggressive, professional sales program was a luxury, not a necessity, in a marketplace characterized by little change and limited competition. Today, banking's marketplace is characterized by major change and intense competition. And the competition is coming from all quarters, not just from other banks. Today, a strong personal selling program is a necessity, not a luxury. Although many senior bank executives recognize the importance of personal selling in their banks, they are not finding this transition an easy one to make. Building an effective, ongoing sales program presents a difficult challenge in institutions that traditionally have been unaggressive in marketing, have looked upon advertising to more or less "make the sale," and have hired people who were attracted to banking in part because of the absence of a selling role.

Today's reality in the banking industry is that strong, bank-wide personal selling capability is both important *and* elusive. We have written this book to assist bank executives in developing or improving the sales program in their banks. Much of the book is based on our research with 10 banks that have made progress in developing their sales programs. We have constructed a framework known as the "Sales Loop Model" based on this research. The Sales Loop Model presents what we consider to be the vital success factors in achieving a first-rate sales program.

Phase I:
The State of the Art

"the industry has a 1950s attitude, 1970s technology, and the
year 2000 needs."

A bank vice president.

Very little empirical research on selling in banks has been conducted to date. Though some material has been published, reviewing one bank's or another's sales program or conceptually
focusing on one or several aspects of bank selling, hard data on
selling in the banking industry are minimal. Phase I of our research was undertaken to fill that information gap—to assess
the "state of the art" in personal selling throughout the banking
industry. We sought to find out where banking is with selling today before focusing on what needs to be done tomorrow.

THE SAMPLE

The sample for the study was 2,000 selected members of the
Bank Marketing Association. Individuals not employed by
banks were excluded from the sample; individuals who were

not the "lead" member for their banks also were excluded to assure that no bank participated in the study more than once.[1]

The overall sample was divided into two 1,000 member subsamples: retail and wholesale. All subjects were mailed the same six-page questionnaire; however, the retail group answered the questions in terms of retail bank selling, and the wholesale group answered in terms of wholesale bank selling.

From the initial mailing and a follow-up mailing, 370 (37%) of the retail sample and 344 (34.4%) of the wholesale sample returned the questionnaires. Most of the 714 respondents were in a senior marketing position in their banks, e.g. vice president of marketing, director of marketing.

The characteristics of the banks participating in the study are shown in Table 2–1. As can be readily seen, the two subsamples are similar on each dimension. Just over 40% of the

TABLE 2-1 ■ Characteristics of Sample Banks

Assets	Retail Sample	Wholesale Sample
$ 49 million and below	16.0%	16.0%
$ 50–$ 99 million	25.0	25.0
$100–$499 million	40.0	40.0
$500 million – $1 billion	7.0	8.0
Above $1 billion	12.0	11.0
Geographic Market Served		
Local	77.0	67.0
Statewide	8.0	8.0
Regional	14.0	22.0
National	0.3	1.5
International	0.8	1.5
Bank's Competitive Strength		
Above Average	65.0	59.0
Average	29.0	32.0
Below Average	6.0	9.0

[1]For a more detailed description of the methodology and findings, see "The State of Personal Selling in Retail Banking," *Journal of Retail Banking*, Fall 1983, pages 1–7; "Personal Selling in Wholesale Banking: A Status Report," *Bankers Magazine*, March–April 1984, pages 39–43; and "The Personal Selling Orientation of Banking in the United States," *International Journal of Bank Marketing*, Volume 2, 1984, pages 12–21.

banks in the total sample have assets under $100 million, with another 40% between $100 million and $500 million. The majority of the banks primarily serve a local geographic market. Well over half of the banks—65% of the retail sample respondents and 59% of the wholesale sample respondents—rated their market position or competitive strength compared to the competition "above average."

THE SALES ORIENTATION INDEX

One of the main objectives of the study was to measure bank's commitment to selling. Our Sales Orientation Index (SOI), shown in Table 2–2, was designed to be such a measurement or barometer.

The SOI's 20 statements were developed based on a review of the literature concerning what is necessary to have a good selling program in banking.[2] Accordingly, included were statements that referred to such areas as senior management support of selling, sales accountabilities, sales training, sales support aids, and sales reward systems.

Respondents rated their banks on each statement using a five-point scale ranging from "Strongly Disagree" (1) to "Strongly Agree" (5). The statements were written so that the higher a bank's total score on the SOI, the more selling-oriented it was thought to be by the respondent. The SOI statements, as well as those in the rest of the questionnaire, were pretested with bankers locally and through a pretest mailing to bankers throughout the country. The SOI also was statistically tested for reliability, with good results. Bank characteristics were analyzed in connection with the SOI to determine if any statistically significant relationships existed.

Table 2–2 compares the retail and wholesale samples' responses to the 20 statements in the SOI. Statistically significant differences, shown in the right-hand column, were found for only four of the statements. In each case, wholesale scores were slightly higher than retail scores. The actual mean differ-

---

[2]Several SOI questions were adapted from Kent Stickler's June 1982 *Journal of Retail Banking* article, "Personal Selling in Retail Banking," Volume 4, pages 74–83.

TABLE 2-2 ■ Means, Standard Deviations, and Test of Significance of Differences in Level of Sales Orientation Between Retail and Wholesale Samples ■■■■■■■■■■■

Items	Retail Mean[a] (S.D.)[b]	Wholesale Mean[a] (S.D.)[b]	t[c]
Organizational Interest in Selling[d]			
1. The organization emphasizes the importance of personal selling from top to bottom.	3.9 (1.1)	3.8 (1.0)	.99
2. Most employees having customer contact responsibilities recognize the importance of sales to the future of the bank.	3.6 (1.0)	3.6 (1.0)	.02
3. The bank's senior management has a personal selling orientation.	3.7 (1.2)	3.7 (1.2)	.11
4. The bank's personnel show an interest in selling the bank's services.	3.0 (0.9)	3.3 (1.0)	.12
5. There is a program for contacting *non-customers* (prospects) for the purpose of making a sales presentation.	3.5 (1.2)	3.7 (1.1)	3.20[h]
6. The bank tailors its personal selling efforts to specific market segments.	3.4 (1.1)	3.4 (1.1)	.59
Overall Scale Mean Score[e]	3.5 (0.8)	3.8 (0.8)	.45
Sales Training			
1. The bank provides sales training on a regular basis.	3.3 (1.2)	3.1 (1.2)	1.70
2. All personnel with the potential for customer contact receive sales training.	3.0 (1.2)	2.9 (1.2)	.59
3. Customer contact personnel are trained in salesmanship techniques, *e.g.* overcoming objections, closing the sale.	3.1 (1.2)	3.1 (1.2)	.04
Overall Scale Mean Score	3.1 (1.1)	3.0 (1.1)	.91
Facilitation of Selling			
1. Bank facilities have been designed to make personal selling easier	3.1 (1.0)	3.0 (1.1)	.19
2. Personal selling efforts are supported with up-to-date information on bank customers.	3.1 (1.1)	3.2 (1.1)	2.05[f]
3. Personal selling efforts are supported with up-to-date information on non-customer prospects.	2.5 (1.0)	2.9 (1.0)	4.79[h]

TABLE 2-2 ■ (concluded)

Items	Retail Mean[a] (S.D.)[b]	Wholesale Mean[a] (S.D.)[b]	t[c]
4. Personal selling efforts are supported by tangible selling aids, for example, sales brochures.	3.8 (1.0)	3.8 (0.9)	.37
Overall Scale Mean Score	3.1 (0.7)	3.2 (0.7)	2.46[g]
Measurement/Accountability/Rewards			
1. Managers with customer responsibilities are accountable for sales results.	3.3 (1.3)	3.1 (1.2)	1.2
2. There is a separate department or person in the organization whose *main* responsibility is overseeing personal selling in the bank.	3.0 (1.4)	3.1 (1.4)	1.30
3. The job descriptions of customer contact personnel clearly communicate the importance of the personal selling role.	3.2 (1.2)	3.3 (1.9)	1.15
4. Outstanding sales performance is an important criterion for "getting ahead" in the bank.	3.2 (1.2)	3.2 (1.1)	.35
5. The record keeping process at the bank allows for measurement of an individual's sales performance	3.0 (1.3)	3.1 (1.2)	1.20
6. Sales performance goals are set for individual personnel having customer contact responsibilities.	2.8 (1.3)	2.8 (1.2)	.54
7. Incentives are used regularly as a means of rewarding personnel who meet or surpass sales goals.	2.7 (1.3)	2.6 (1.2)	.88
Overall Scale Mean Score	3.0 (1.0)	3.0 (0.8)	.60

[a]The overall mean score was computed by dividing the sum of the item mean scores in a grouping by the number of items.

[b]SD = standard deviation

[c]t = statistical "t" test which indicates if there is a statistical difference in the retail and wholesale means.

[d]Only the individual items appeared on the questionnaire. The categories "organizational interest in selling," "sales training," "facilitation of selling," and "measurement/accountability/rewards" did not appear on the questionnaire. These categories are the result of a statistical factor analyses performed and the researchers' own interpretations.

[e]For each item, respondents used a scale ranging from "strongly disagree" (1 point) to "strongly agree" (5 points). The item mean score represents the average score for all respondents on that item. The higher the item score, the more respondents agreed with the statement.

[f]$p = .04$

[g]$p = .01$

[h]$p = .001$

ences are so few and small they may have occurredd by chance. In any case, the similarities in the status of personal selling in retail banking and of personal selling in wholesale banking are far more striking than the differences.

The data in Table 2–2 also suggest that, at this time, tangible implementation of bank selling programs lags behind the recognition that bank employees do indeed need to sell. Statements grouped under the category "organizational interest in selling" had overall means of 3.5 and 3.8 for the retail and wholesale samples, respectively. Response to the first statement in this category indicates that selling *is* receiving emphasis in banking organizations. Yet the response to the fourth statement indicates that bank contact personnel show much less enthusiasm for selling.

The overall means for "sales training," "facilitation of selling," and "measurement/accountability/rewards"—categories generally referring to specific actions in support of selling effectiveness—underscore the discrepancy between interest in selling and actual efforts to improve selling. The scale means for these latter three categories range from 3.0 to 3.1, the midpoint of the 1-5 scale. Several individual statements have means below 3.0, indicating that most banks are doing little in these areas.

Table 2–3 summarizes how the banks did on the SOI in general. The higher the score, the more sales-oriented the bank, with 100 being the highest possible score (a rating of 5 on each of the 20 items). These SOI data can be used as a barometer of personal selling's state of development in U.S. banks belonging to the Bank Marketing Association, and from them three broad groupings seem to emerge: (1) banks that have already made substantial progress in building selling programs (the banks with scores above 80); (2) banks that have made some progress but still have much developmental work to do (the banks between 80 and 60), and (3) banks that have done little or nothing to develop a sales program (the banks scoring below 60). A score below 60 means there is more disagreement than agreement with the SOI statements, as 60 is right at the midpoint of possible scores. That over one-third of the sample banks scored below 60 indicates that personal selling is far from being a mature function in U.S. banks in the mid-1980s.

TABLE 2-3 ■ Sales Orientation Index

SOI Scores[a]	Retail Sample[b]		Wholesale Sample[c]	
	Number	Percent	Number	Percent
90 and above	20	5.4%	11	3.2%
80–89	50	13.5	44	12.8
70–79	66	17.8	80	23.3
60–69	96	26.0	92	26.7
Below 60	138	37.3	117	34.0
Total	370	100.0%	344	100.0%

[a]Each banks sales orientation score was computed by totaling the rating of the 20 individual SOI items. A perfect score would be 100 based upon a rating of "Strongly Agree" (5 points) on each of the 20 items.
[b]All retail banks SOI = 64
[c]All wholesale banks SOI = 65

Cross-classifying SOI scores among various breakdowns of the sample banks, reveals several statistically significant relationships. Banks that are primarily wholesale banks or that give equal emphasis to retail and wholesale banking had a significantly higher average SOI score (67) than did primarily retail banks (62). Banks rated as above average in market position or competitive strength had a significantly higher score (67) than banks rated as below average (57). There was a tendency for larger banks to have higher SOI scores. This trend, however, was not statistically significant. The data suggest that larger banks have not led smaller institutions in terms of personal selling innovation.

SALES TRAINING INDEX

Another facet of this study concerned the extent and level of sales training among U.S. banks. Among the questions guiding this part of the research: Just how developed is the sales training function in banking? Are larger banks more advanced in training than smaller banks? Are salespersons calling on corporate prospects exposed to more sales training than personnel selling to consumers? In which particular training areas do banks invest most heavily?

FIGURE 2-1 ■ Bank Sales Training Model

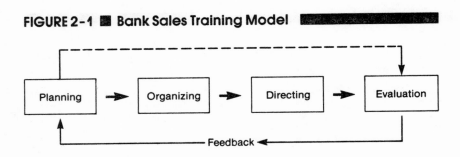

The sales training model shown in Figure 2–1 aided us in the design of this part of the research. The model is divided into four phases: planning, organizing, directing, and evaluation. Planning involves organizational analysis (relating sales training to the firm's objectives), operational analysis (considering job descriptions in designing sales training), and salesperson analysis (determining the needed sales behavior).

The recommendation that the planning phase be closely associated with the evaluation phase (Futrell 1981) is indicated in the model by the broken line connecting the two phases. It is important to develop specific training goals (e.g. increase in sales, call/order ratio) and to evaluate the results of sales training. Program goals should be compared to actual results. This step helps to determine the "bottom line" effectiveness of sales training.

Organizing sales training involves funding specific training programs, providing the necessary facilities. etc. Directing sales training involves the actual conduct of the training, the skills of the trainers, their attitudes, etc.

Included in the questionnaire sent to our study sample were 20 statements comprising a Sales Training Index (STI). The STI is a measure of the level of sales training efforts in a given bank. The STI's 20 statements concern the four elements in the sales training model shown in Figure 2–1. Respondents rated their banks on these statements using a five-point scale ranging from "Strongly Disagree" (1) to "Strongly Agree" (5). The higher the bank's total score, the higher the level of sales training in the bank as perceived by the respondent. The maximum possible score was 100, *i.e.* a score of 5 on each of the 20 items.

Although the total sample was 370 retail respondents and 344 wholesale respondents, the sales training questions, including the 20-item STI, were completed only by the 234 retail and 220 wholesale respondents whose banks had sales training programs. Thirty-six percent of the retail banks and 35 percent of the wholesale banks did *not* have a sales training program at the time of the study.

Findings on Sales Training

One purpose of the study was to determine if wholesale banks were emphasizing sales training more than retail banks. As shown in Table 2–4, no significant difference between the two groups was found on either responses to the STI's individual questions or the overall means of its three scales. Also revealed by Table 2–4 are higher overall mean scores for "Organizing" (3.5, 3.5) and "Directing" (3.7, 3.7) than for "Planning and Evaluation" (3.2, 3.1).

The total scores on the STI for the retail and wholesale sample banks are presented in Table 2–5. Each bank's sales training score was computed by totaling the ratings for each of the 20 STI items. Shown by Table 2–5 is that just over 50% of both subsamples either scored below 60, indicating more overall disagreement than agreement with the 20 statements, or did not do any sales training at all. Only 15 percent of the retail sample and 13 percent of the wholesale sample scored above the 80 mark. The average STI scores for the wholesale and retail samples (69 and 67 respectively) were not significantly different.

A common assumption is that larger, more geographically diverse banks are more advanced in their sales training than smaller banks. However, there is no statistical difference between the STI of local banks (Mean = 68.2) and banks serving a statewide, regional, national, or international market (Mean = 68.7). Furthermore, no significant differences were found when statistical comparisons of STI scores were made based on bank asset size.

TABLE 2-4 ■ Means, Standard Deviations, and Test of Significance of Differences in the Level of Sales Training Between Retail and Wholesale Samples

Item	Retail Mean (S.D.) n = 234	Wholesale Mean (S.D.) n = 220	t
Planning and Evaluation			
1. Job descriptions for our sales positions are considered when developing sales training programs.	3.2 (1.0)	3.2 (1.0)	.11
2. We have specific goals which our sales training program is expected to meet.	3.2 (1.1)	3.2 (1.0)	.02
3. Sales training goals are related directly to the goals of the bank.	3.5 (1.0)	3.5 (0.9)	.29
4. We analyze our salespeople's job in order to determine their sales training needs.	3.3 (1.0)	3.4 (1.0)	.47
5. We regularly evaluate the results of our sales training programs.	3.2 (1.1)	3.2 (1.0)	.12
6. At the same time sales training goals are determined, methods are established to evaluate the effectiveness of the training.	2.9 (1.0)	3.0 (0.9)	.51
7. We use specific items (increase in sales, call/order ratio) to evaluate sales training results.	3.0 (1.1)	2.9 (1.0)	.75
8. Information used for evaluating the sales training program is gathered before and after training takes place.	3.0 (1.0)	2.9 (1.0)	.78
Overall Scale Mean Score	3.2 (0.8)	3.1 (0.8)	.48
Organizing			
1. Sales training takes place on a regular basis in our bank.	3.5 (1.0)	3.4 (1.0)	.93
2. Management provides the necessary budget for sales training.	3.5 (1.1)	3.5 (1.0)	.30
3. Most bank personnel in selling roles seem to make use of the information provided them in sales training sessions.	3.6 (0.8)	3.5 (0.8)	1.81

TABLE 2-4 ■ (concluded)

Item	Retail Mean (S.D.) n = 234	Wholesale Mean (S.D.) n = 220	t
4. We have good sales training facilities.	3.3 (1.1)	3.3 (1.0)	.53
5. The bank's management supports the sales training program.	3.9 (0.8)	3.8 (0.8)	1.10
6. The degree of managerial support for the sales training program is recognized by the bank's staff.	3.6 (0.9)	3.5 (0.9)	.71
7. The bank's sales training program motivates our employees to want sales success.	3.3 (0.8)	3.1 (0.9)	1.63
Overall Scale Mean Score	3.5 (0.71)	3.5 (0.74)	1.13
Directing			
1. Sales training is performed in a positive manner that encourages our salespeople.	3.8 (0.8)	3.8 (0.8)	.60
2. The personnel who lead our sales training sessions have the necessary background and experience.	3.6 (0.9)	3.6 (0.9)	.05
3. There is an individual or department in our bank responsible for developing and coordinating sales training programs.	3.8 (0.9)	3.8 (0.9)	.34
4. The personnel who lead our sales training sessions are effective in communicating salesmanship techniques to others.	3.7 (0.8)	3.6 (0.9)	.87
5. The personnel who conduct our sales training are themselves skilled sales people.	3.4 (1.0)	3.4 (1.0)	.74
Overall Scale Mean Score	3.7 (0.74)	3.7 (0.77)	.63

TABLE 2-5 ■ Sales Training Index

Sales Training Scores[a]	Retail Sample[b]		Wholesale Sample[c]	
	Number	Percent	Number	Percent
90 and above	16	4.3%	12	3.5%
80–89	41	11.1	32	9.3
70–79	65	17.6	64	18.6
60–69	61	16.5	51	14.8
Below 60	54	14.6	65	18.9
No training	133	35.9	120	34.9
Total	370	100.0%	344	100.0%

[a]Each banks sales training score was computed by totaling the rating of the 20 individual items. A perfect score would be 100 based upon a rating of "Strongly Agree" (5 points) on each of the 20 items.
[b]All retail banks STI = 67
[c]All wholesale banks STI = 69

Allocation of Time in Training

The sample banks were asked to indicate the proportion of time devoted to different skill and knowledge areas in contact personnel training. As can be clearly seen in Table 2–6, far more time is devoted to knowledge development than skill development. Approximately half of total training time is spent on product information (the bank's services and the competitors'). Relatively little time is devoted to specific salesmanship tech-

TABLE 2-6 ■ Percentage of Time Spent in Bank's Training for Customer Contact Personnel

	Retail	Wholesale
Information about bank's products	41%	39%
Information about competitors' products	9	8
Bank's marketing program	16	16
Information about customers and prospects	11	12
Specific salesmanship techniques	15	17
Other (operations, policies, daily job duties)	8	8

niques. Again, the similarities among the retail and wholesale samples are striking.

Priorities for Improving Sales Training

Participants in this study also were asked to indicate the most important priorities for improving sales training in their banks. The results are shown in Table 2–7. Over one-third of the respondents from both sub-samples referred to improving the training curriculum, e.g. product knowledge training, sales skills training, sales management training. Over 20 percent of both samples mentioned improving the support of training, which would include increasing the training budget. Priorities were similar for both samples.

TABLE 2-7 ■ Important Priorities for Improving Sales Training

Response Category	Retail Sample Frequency	Retail Sample Percent[a]	Wholesale Sample Frequency	Wholesale Sample Percent[a]
Improve training curriculum	134	36.2%	128	37.2%
Improve support of training	83	22.4	74	21.5
Increase motivation to sell	68	18.4	65	18.9
Measure/evaluate training	42	11.3	39	11.3
Provide time to train	26	7.0	15	4.4
Train throughout bank	15	4.0	4	1.2
Incorporate effective learning methods	19	5.1	25	7.3
Miscellaneous	79	21.4	56	16.3
Total	466		406	

[a]In this table the percentages do not total 100% because respondents could provide more than one response. The percentage figures should be read as: 36.2% of the retail respondents cited improving the training curriculum as one of the important priorities.

BIGGEST PROBLEMS IN DEVELOPING A SALES PROGRAM

An open-ended question in the survey asked the respondents to indicate the biggest problems in developing an effective sales program for their banks. This question was related to selling in general, not just to sales training. The responses to this question, summarized in Table 2–8, again reveal few differences between the retail and wholesale samples.

Over one-third of the respondents in both samples mentioned insufficient managerial commitment, which includes insufficient budgets and staff. One respondent wrote: "We need a consistent direction from senior management. Our sales training is an 'on-again, off-again' approach. The trainers are highly competent but frustrated by changing signals." Another banker wrote: "The individual responsible for the development

TABLE 2-8 ■ Biggest Problems in Developing an Effective Selling Program

Response Category	Retail Sample		Wholesale Sample	
	Frequency	Percent[a]	Frequency	Percent[a]
Lack of Management Commitment	128	34.6%	123	36%
Contact Personnel Do Not Have Right Orientation/ Attitude	117	31.6	94	27
Insufficient Time To Sell	91	24.6	68	20
Poor Sales Management	56	15.1	53	15
Inadequate Training	53	14.3	43	13
Problems Measuring/ Evaluating Sales Results	34	9.2	39	11
Inadequate Incentives	30	8.1	29	8
Difficulty in Maintaining Momentum	13	3.5	19	6
Inadequate Sales Aids	11	3.0	12	3
Miscellaneous	62	16.8	40	12
Total	595		520	

[a]In this table the percentages do not total 100% because respondents could provide more than one response. The percentage figures should be read as: 34.6% of the retail respondents cited lack of commitment as one of the biggest problems.

of the selling program wears too many hats. This should be a dedicated responsibility."

Just under one-third of the respondents referred to the orientation and attitudes of contact personnel as a big problem. One banker wrote: "Employees' basic attitude is that selling is a dirty word. We're still 'order-takers' instead of salespeople." Another respondent said: "Employees have been hired based on their skill or aptitude with 'numbers'—not based on skill or aptitude with people. Having the right personnel is the key." Another banker wrote: "We need to hire new salespeople and pay according to performance. We all are trying to make salespeople out of the present staff, and these people are just not salespeople."

One-fourth of respondents mentioned the problem of insufficient time to sell. One put it this way: "So far, it has been mainly talk and no action. Overloading people and not letting them make an honest effort in their areas of responsibility."

What we see is that the problems bankers face in developing an effective sales program directly relate to the ratings of their banks' sales orientation. The management support and budgets to actually implement a well-rounded sales program are frequently perceived to be insufficient, contributing to the "more talk than action" profile showing through in the SOI data. The absence of tangible "action," such as a control system for measuring sales goal attainment, in turn does little to improve the sales orientation or attitude of contact personnel, many of whom have never before been asked by their banks to sell.

PRIORITIES FOR IMPROVING SELLING EFFECTIVENESS

A question in the survey also asked participants to indicate the most important priorities for increasing selling effectiveness in their banks. Responses to this question are summarized in Table 2–9.

By a large margin, sales training was most frequently mentioned as a priority, with 38% of the respondents from both samples referring to it. The second most frequently mentioned priority was providing rewards/incentives for selling. Some respondents combined these areas of need; others focused on them separately. The following comments are examples:

- "We need an attitude change to a 'selling-oriented way of thinking.' We need to train these people and then measure performance and reward them accordingly."
- "We need to structure a training program for all employees: (1) what a bank is and does; (2) jobs in the bank; (3) product knowledge; (4) customer needs and wants; (5) sell, sell, sell."
- "Training. A structured program needs to be developed. An effective monitoring program with success tied to career advancement is needed."
- "Compensation! . . . As soon as the reward program is finalized, we are ready."

Again, the items contained in the last three categories of the SOI are stressed. Tables 2–8 and 2–9 together reveal that bank marketers overseeing their banks' sales programs perceive the need to improve factors relating to sales planning, management, training, and measurement/rewards/incentives.

TABLE 2-9 ■ Mosts Important Priorities for Increasing Selling Effectiveness

Response Category	Retail Sample		Wholesale Sample	
	Frequency	Percent	Frequency	Percent
Sales training	139	38%	129	38%
Rewards/incentives for selling	67	18	55	16
Sales management	57	15	45	13
Support of sales program[a]	51	14	38	11
Develop employee sales attitudes	50	13	27	8
Measure sales performance	28	8	30	9
Sales aids	19	5	21	6
Time to sell	16	4	8	2
Establish call/sale program	13	3	12	3
Miscellaneous	90	24	82	24
Total	530		447	

[a]Includes adequate budgets, qualified staff, managerial support.

CONCLUSION

The data from Phase I of this study show that managerial interest in improving bank selling performance and managerial commitment to "making it happen" are not the same thing. Many banks in the sample appear to be in the "talking about selling" stage at this time. Specific actions actually taken tend to be the easier, less costly, or less disruptive ones, e.g. providing contact personnel with sales pamphlets and brochures. Investment in better *sales skills* (through training), in better *sales support* (through prospect information and the right kind of facilities), and in better *sales motivation* (through a system of measurements, accountabilities, and rewards) lags behind. Echoing the comments of many others, one respondent wrote: "Senior management has not made the commitment to train the staff, hire sales-oriented people, or set goals and pay incentives."

The retail and wholesale sub-samples had essentially the same performance on the SOI. What this means is that, overall, the development of personal selling is no more advanced on the wholesale side of banking than on the retail side. However, when all of the sample banks are categorized by the markets they *emphasize*, significantly different SOI scores do result. Banks emphasizing the retail market had a significantly lower SOI score than banks giving equal or more attention to wholesale markets. Also, banks rated as above average in competitive strength had a higher SOI score than banks rated as below average.

Since one can assume that banks belonging to the Bank Marketing Association have a greater interest in marketing than banks that are not members, the SOI scores for the sample banks (drawn from the BMA membership roster) are undoubtedly higher than they would be for a sample drawn from all banks in the United States.

Approximately 36 percent of the sample banks have no sales training program whatsoever. That is an amazing statistic! Again, since the sample was drawn from the membership roster of the Bank Marketing Association, it is likely that an even higher percentage of all banks in the United States have no sales training program. The assumption is that membership in BMA signifies some degree of interest in marketing within a bank.

Clearly, U.S. banks have a long road ahead of them in terms of developing solid sales training programs. The aggregate scores on the Sales Training Index can be considered somewhat low given that fewer than 15 percent of the banks in the sample scored over 80 (out of a possible score of 100) and that not one of the 20 STI items achieved an average score of 4.0 or above (out of a possible 5) from either the retail or wholesale samples. The scores for "planning and evaluation" items were especially low, hovering around the 3.0–3.2 range for the most part.

Data from other questions reinforce the low-level sales training profile that emerges from the STI results. That "lack of management commitment" was the most frequently mentioned problem in developing an effective selling program clearly relates to the unaggressive approach to sales training that shows through in this research. Successful sales training requires resources and continuity, and these in turn require senior management commitment to building a sales organization. The second most frequently mentioned problem, "contact personnel orientation/attitude" undoubtedly stems, in part, from sales training program deficiencies. Motivation to sell is related to one's preparedness to sell.

Bank marketing personnel do recognize the importance of sales training in their banks. Far and away the most important priority for increasing selling effectiveness in the sample banks was sales training. Nearly 40 percent of the retail and wholesale sample respondents mentioned sales training when asked about priorities in an open-ended question that could have elicited any type of response.

When the data from various questions are combined, bank marketer respondents—whether they are referring to the retail or wholesale sides of their banks—are saying, in effect: (1) Personal selling is important to our success; (2) we are not effectively training our people; (3) we have problems getting support from upper management; (4) many of our personnel are not, or do not want to be, sales-oriented; and (5) sales training should be a top priority.

3

Phase II: Identifying Success Factors

"The customer relationship
. . . begins with the sale."

Kenneth A. Meyers, "The Selling Professional of the 1980s." Business, *October–December 1982, p. 44.*

We expected that banks achieving success in developing sales programs would have certain attributes in common. We conducted Phase II of the research to determine if this assumption was correct and, if so, to identify these attributes. Identifying the key "success factors" in developing a sales program, and learning more about the realities involved in achieving them, would enable us to share this knowledge with the banking industry as a whole.

The basis of Phase II was an in-depth study of 10 U.S. banks that appeared to us to have made considerable progress in establishing a sales program. We had surveyed a large sample of banks in Phase I to acquire an overall sense of the "state of the art" in bank sales programs. In Phase II, our interest was to dig deeper to find out what advanced selling banks had done to become advanced. To dig deeper—to learn facts, nuances, details—we visited each of the 10 banks, interviewing numerous bank personnel and reviewing various materials.

SELECTING THE SAMPLE BANKS

Selecting the 10 banks for the sample was clearly one of the most important steps in the entire study. Our objective was not to identify the 10 "best" selling banks in America, which for all intents and purposes would have been impossible. Rather, our intent was to identify 10 banks that had made substantial progress in developing a sales program. This is an important distinction and one about which we wish to be very clear.

With approximately 15,000 banks in the United States as we write this book, we know that many banks not included in our sample have sales programs equal to or possibly even better than the sales programs of the banks in the sample. We do not, however, view this as a weakness of the research. As our objective was to isolate the key success factors in developing a sales program, our need was to find banks to study that have successful programs. We did not need to find the "10 best" to accomplish what we set out to accomplish.

Our sample of 10 banks is strictly a judgment sample. We did not use an exacting scientific process to select them. We based the selections on our own assessments of banks with which we were familiar, on the recommendations of Phase I respondents who listed on their questionnaires up to three banks thought to be doing a good job in personal selling, and on the suggestions of bankers and consultants around the country whose opinions we solicited. Another influencing factor was our desire to achieve reasonable geographic and asset size balance in the sample. Finally, we were influenced by our interest in studying the "wholesale" sales programs in half of the banks, and the "retail" sales programs in the other half. Thus, we ultimately selected banks to be in either wholesale or retail subsamples. It turned out that we had six retail and four wholesale sample banks. The reason is that one of the original wholesale sample banks proved to have a stronger retail sales program, so we studied their retail program instead.

Nine of the 10 banks invited to participate in the study accepted. Another bank was selected to replace the one that declined to participate. Although the 10 sample banks differed in the maturity and sophistication of their sales programs, all can be considered well above banking industry norms in the progress they have made to date. The sales programs of some of the sample banks are likely as outstanding as those of any bank in the United States.

The banks participating in the study are listed below. Table 3–1, "Profile of Sample Banks Year-End 1983," provides additional details.

Retail Sample	*Wholesale Sample*
C & S National Bank of South Carolina	Fleet National Bank
Friendly National Bank	Sunwest Bank of Albuquerque
Landmark Bank of Orlando	Wachovia Bank & Trust Company
Louisiana National Bank	Wells Fargo Bank
Security Pacific National Bank	
Worthen Bank and Trust Company	

THE INTERVIEWS

We interviewed a total of 147 people in our visits to the 10 banks. In each bank we sought to interview the CEO or president, the senior manager of the wholesale or retail bank (whichever was appropriate), the marketing director, other marketing department personnel involved in the sales program, human resources personnel involved in the sales program, sales managers, and salespeople. We conducted group interviews with sales managers and salespeople and individual interviews with everyone else.

Participants in the group interviews were always homogeneous, e.g. a group of branch managers or a group of commercial calling officers. Group interviews generally involved two to five respondents and typically lasted between one and one-half and two hours. Individual interviews generally lasted from an hour to an hour and one-half.

We developed separate interview guides for the group and the individual interviews, although certain questions appeared on both guides. The questions were open-ended and designed to stimulate in-depth discussion of the issues at hand. Our technique was to probe for as much information as possible and to

TABLE 3-1 ■ Profile of Sample Banks Year-End 1983 ($ thousands)

Bank Name	Headquarters	Holding Company Affiliation	Assets	Deposits	Number of Domestic Branches
C & S National Bank of South Carolina	Columbia, South Carolina	The Citizens and Southern Corporation	$ 1,767,297	$ 1,406,477	125
Fleet National Bank	Providence, Rhode Island	The Fleet Financial Group	4,866,012	3,542,902	46
Friendly National Bank	Oklahoma City, Oklahoma	None	135,000	118,000	None
Landmark Bank of Orlando	Orlando, Florida	Landmark Banking Corp. of Florida	72,763	67,298	3
Louisiana National Bank	Baton Rouge, Louisiana	First Bancshares of Louisiana	997,248	837,233	27
Security Pacific National Bank	Los Angeles, California	Security Pacific Corporation	36,098,916	27,763,181	625
Sunwest Bank of Albuquerque	Albuquerque, New Mexico	Sunwest Financial Services	1,281,258	1,079,890	24
Wachovia Bank and Trust Company	Winston-Salem, North Carolina	Wachovia Corporation	7,690,766	5,825,768	202
Wells Fargo Bank	Oakland, California	Wells Fargo & Company	23,800,000	22,700,000	373
Worthen Bank and Trust Company	Little Rock, Arkansas	First Arkansas Bankstock Corp.	782,583	565,805	16

follow up general or vague responses by asking for clarification or more details. We asked two questions of all respondents:

1. What are the main reasons that _____ Bank apparently has been more successful in building a sales program than most banks around the country?
2. Are there aspects of your sales program you would like to see improved?

In addition to these and other questions we frequently asked, we queried selected individuals about their specialty. For example, we would devote much of our interview time with a training coordinator to a discussion of the bank's sales training philosophy and program.

All respondents were promised anonymity to encourage candor. For this reason, the many verbatim quotations we use in the book are not attributed to an individual by name. Instead, we attribute quotes to "a bank executive," "a calling officer," etc.

We learned a great deal about what was actually occurring in a bank's sales program by virtue of being "outsiders," by promising anonymity, by using open-ended questions and probing techniques, by asking certain questions of everyone, and by interviewing employees at all levels of the organization structure rather than focusing on one level or another. What we learned is fascinating. We share these insights in the pages that follow.

THE SALES LOOP MODEL

The central conclusion from our Phase II research is that the concept of sales success factors as a prerequisite for a productive sales program is valid. Again and again in our bank visits and interviews, we found the same factors keying a bank's success with its sales program. And when we found significant weaknesses in a bank's overall program, these weaknesses were invariably traceable to deficiencies with one or more of the success factors.

Through our in-depth study of 10 bank sales programs, we identified nine sales success factors. They are presented in Figure 3–1, "The Sales Loop Model."

We use the phrase *Sales Loop Model* because the task of developing a sustained, professional, and proactive sales pro-

FIGURE 3-1 ■ The Sales Loop Model

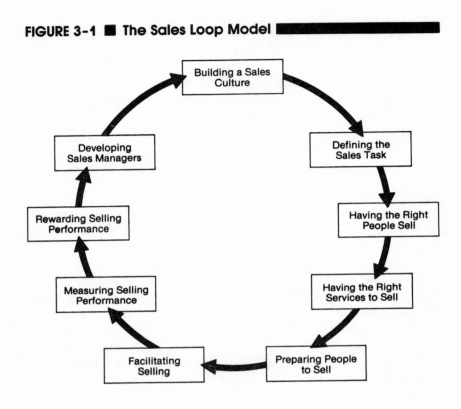

gram involves multiple, critical steps, each essential in laying the proper foundation. No magic answer or easy approach to a successful sales program is available. A sequence of nine key elements must be put into place. The elements are ongoing rather than discrete. That is, they require continuous development and refinement and attention. Weakness in just one element will keep a bank from fully realizing its potential as a selling institution. A bank needs to be strong in all nine areas. *It needs to close the sales loop and keep it closed!*

In Chapters 4 through 12 we "build" the sales loop, element by element. These chapters are the heart of the book. We attempt to bolster the word-picture of the sales loop with insight into the true meaning of the words appearing in the connected boxes. In so doing, we hope to provide the reader with the blueprint for developing a new sales program or improving an existing one.

Part Two

THE
SALES
LOOP

4

Building a
Sales Culture

> "businesses are human institutions, not plush buildings, bottom lines, strategic analysis, or five-year plans."
>
> *Terrence E. Deal and Allan A. Kennedy,* Corporate Cultures, *p. 4.*

A sales culture, more than any other element, is part and parcel of the entire sales loop! With a strong sales culture, everything involved in the selling program is easier; without it, genuine progress in developing a sales program is virtually impossible.

Culture defines what is important in an organization. It is the attitudes and behaviors to which most members of an organization subscribe. It both shapes and is shaped by an organization's inner dynamics: management deeds, not just management words; behavior that is rewarded; projects that win approval and funding. Culture is intangible, but powerful. No organization is without a culture.

Building a sales culture in banks that have traditionally paid little attention to selling—or rejected it outright—is a difficult and protracted enterprise. It cannot be accomplished in a bank whose management is superficially committed to a selling philosophy.

Cultural change is an act of undoing and dismantling as much as it is an act of creating (Biggart, 1977). For many banks

■ **The Sales Loop** ▐████████████████████████████▌

```
┌─────────────────┐
│ Building a Sales │
│     Culture      │
└─────────────────┘
```

the task is one of converting bank personnel who have never before held a "sales" position—and who may have entered the banking profession to avoid such a position—into capable, professional, and motivated salespeople. The task is one of moving human beings from anti-selling, neutral-selling, or even mildly positive selling attitudes and behaviors to *pro-selling* attitudes and behaviors. The task, simply put, is to get selling into the organization's *bloodstream*.

CHARACTERISTICS OF A SALES CULTURE

Most of the banks in our sample have a true sales culture; the remaining banks are making progress toward one. We have identified six characteristics of a true sales culture. Readers are encouraged to consider the presence or absence of these characteristics in their own institutions when evaluating the state of development of the institution's sales culture.

1. Customer orientation. The sample banks with the strongest sales cultures are genuinely customer-oriented and have been for an extended period of time. Sales is viewed as a way to satisfy the customer's needs, as a way to help the customer. Sales is viewed as a way to *serve*.

People we interviewed repeatedly referred to the customer in their responses. They spoke of putting the customer first; of treating *all* customers well, not just upscale customers; of being highly responsive to customer problems and complaints. One of the sample banks has a "sundown" rule, which is to respond to a customer complaint before the sun goes down on the day the complaint is received. Another sample bank has established a centralized function called "action central" to handle promptly customer inquiries and problems over the telephone.

The following quotations are representative of the customer-oriented attitudes we heard reflected many times in the course of our interviews:

"The customer is not an interruption to our work, but the cause of our work." (*new accounts representative*)

"Our customers perceive we want to lend them money, that we want the business." (*calling officer*)

"When we screw up, we make it five times right. We over-compensate." (*credit card manager*)

"We try to give the same service to the little guy as we do to the bigger customer. It's part of our philosophy. Customers feel like they are important even when they are small. The repeat business has astounded me. We have fathers, sons, and so forth who keep banking with us." (*consumer loan officer*)

"You have to go out and see the customer's machines and treat him well, even if he wears overalls. We have people in our community with cow _____ on their shoes who could buy or sell any of us." (*branch manager*)

"Our emphasis is not on our quota or dollar amounts; it's on the customer's needs. We don't high-pressure. We don't believe in it." (*new accounts representative*)

"We have been able to maintain the personal attention in spite of growth. Our customers are aware that we will make time for them if they need it. This builds customer loyalty. Our customers do a good job selling the bank to others." (*branch manager*)

2. Pervasive selling attitude. The attitude that selling is both legitimate and important reaches throughout the organization in the sample banks with the strongest sales cultures. Virtually everyone we spoke with in these banks are "believers": top management, line division managers, commercial lenders, supervisors, branch personnel, staff officers. In these organizations, selling is religion. Serious religion, not fanatical religion. There is belief in the idea that selling behavior is vital to the bank's future; in the idea that every bank employee needs to sell; in the idea that the bank has to go after business, not wait for it.

We fondly refer to one of our sample banks as the "fireman's bank." The following quotation explains: "Our guards sell our bank. They know all customers by name. Several are ex-fire chiefs. Now all the firemen in town bank here." A loan officer at this same bank said: "When I first started here, I saw myself strictly as a loan officer. Being around here, I have come to see myself as a salesperson."

3. Sense of "team." The banks having the strongest sales cultures have sales offices, or sales groups, not just salespeople. The emphasis on team sales goals (as well as individual sales goals) and on team sales success is clearly evident.

A number of the sample banks regularly hold sales meetings to share information, publicly recognize top performers, put pressure on those who are not carrying their fair share of the load, and, in general, foster the sense of team. The group responsible for merchant credit card and ATM network sales in one sample bank meets every Monday morning. Every salesperson reports all calls made the previous week. The reasons for rejections and strategies for overcoming them are discussed. Minutes of the meetings are distributed to each participant.

The manager of the cash management department of a sample bank holds a sales meeting every Friday morning. The meetings last two hours. Product managers and operations managers attend, in addition to sales personnel. Salespeople in the field participate via a conference call hookup. Salespeople comment about what customers and prospects are saying and what the competition is doing. If it's reported that a competitor has come out with a new idea or service, the group attempts to decide there and then whether to respond and, if so, how. A key purpose of these meetings is to keep everyone informed. Another is to decide on a quick response to marketplace opportunities and threats. Another is to develop a greater sense of partnership between those selling the service and those delivering it.

Most of the salespeople we spoke with during the study felt a part of something; they did not feel alone in the sales role. When asked why the bank had been successful in selling, one salesperson said simply: "We are family." From another banker: "I've worked at several banks, and the attitude here toward customers and the family feeling among employees is unique."

4. Institutional pride. Respondents in our study believed in their banks. They feel they work for the best bank in their marketplace; they feel they work for a "winner" institution. They are proud and loyal, unlikely to leave the bank for another. We repeatedly heard comments like the following:

- "We are No. 1; we are the best."
- "We set the pace for just about everything."
- "I'm so proud of what we're doing. When I took a seminar in Chicago [on selling], I learned that we were already doing everything."

One result of institutional pride is that salespeople are inclined to sell the bank and to sell *for* the bank, not just to sell for themselves. Another result is a deeply rooted concern for excellence. In one sample bank, generally regarded as one of the best-managed banks in America, the top four managers in the corporate bank meet quarterly in an "improvement" session. One of these managers remarked: "We focus on what's not working. Coming out of a session like this, you would think the bank was in real trouble. It's bloody." In another bank thousands of miles away, the cash management department had recently remodeled its offices because, as the manager put it: "the offices looked bad, and I felt this is not how the 'best' looks."

Still another result of institutional pride is peer group pressure to perform. Selling expectations tended to be high in the sample banks, and most of the salespeople we interviewed were acutely aware of keeping up with their peers. One banker said, in the context of sales performance: "In this bank, you are more worried about the peer group than the boss. You don't want to be perceived by peers as a low performer." Another employee in the same bank stated: "If you are not successful, your peers know it. There is a sense of urgency." At a different bank, the marketing director discussing peer pressure commented that it is ". . . almost like going back to high school." A loan officer at still another bank said: "People here expect you to do your best—and then some—and this is the norm."

5. Visible top management commitment. Employees believe top management's commitment to selling is *real* in the sample banks having the strongest sales cultures. Top-level managers set a sales example through their own behavior by making sales calls themselves or by assisting on calls; by insisting on sales performance as a criterion for customer contact employees advancing in the bank; and, in general, by "biting the bullet" and making the necessary investments for the sales program to have "teeth."

Our research underscores the conclusion of Silverzweig and Allen (1976), who wrote:

> An organization's culture is tremendously influenced by the behavior of the people with the most authority and power. Behavior throughout the organization is affected not by what top management pays lip service to, nor even by what it actually does, but rather by what leaders are perceived as doing, by what appears to get their attention and their priority.

How senior managers spend their time, what they support, what they genuinely care about, is critical in culture development. In one sample bank's call program, the president presides over the monthly sales meeting. The president's involvement has had a telling impact on sales culture development in this bank. However, during a recent period, other priorities won out and the "monthly" meeting became less regular. This, too, had a cultural impact—but not in the desired direction. Clearly, actions speak louder than words in culture development.

At another sample bank, a senior manager stated: "We probably make more senior management calls than any bank in the United States. One responsibility of calling officers is to make sure senior management gets to see our top accounts in the corporate bank once a year. This is important. A corporate treasurer knows how a bank works and knows the calling officer is not on the loan committee. We want our large accounts to perceive they have a link into the inner circle of the bank." A calling officer in this same bank remarked: "Culture is visible here. The CEO demonstrates the culture through his actions. You have to shut your eyes not to see it."

In brief, management has strong convictions about the need for selling, and everyone in the bank knows of these convictions in the best selling programs. Consider the following statements from various banks in the sample:

> "Senior management told us this is what we're going to do; this is the way it's going to be. They were 150 percent behind the (sales) program from its beginning and we knew it. They have continued to support it. They have gone along with all of our suggestions on improving the program." (sales coordinator)

> "Our people know this [officer call program] is the president's project, his baby." (call program coordinator)

> "You must sell to make it here. Management will know or make a point to find out." (branch manager)

> "The president is one of the best salesmen you could have. He is a pretty good role model around here. He is fulfilling a leadership role." (loan officer)

> "The chairman and president of the bank think [selling] is important. As a result, everyone else thinks it's important." (marketing director)

6. Faith in employees. A final characteristic of a sales culture is that top management has a fundamental faith in the ability and willingness of existing employees to sell if given the proper tools and encouragement. Instead of the notion that the bank's employees can't or won't sell is the notion that they can and will sell under the proper conditions. The top managers we spoke with recognized that some personnel were not cut out for sales for one reason or another. Nevertheless, they considered the employee group as a whole as capable of selling—and selling well. One senior executive made the point this way: "I have a very, very strong feeling about the capability of our people from top to bottom. They are responsive. They are willing to learn. They are willing to expand their horizons."

Taken together, these six characteristics of a sales culture form a basis for understanding its essential character. Culture represents the central attitudes and behaviors of a group, the behaviors a reflection of the attitudes. In the six characteristics we see attitudes that lead to sales behavior:

1. An attitude of helping and satisfying the customer.
2. An attitude that selling helps the customer and the bank.
3. An attitude that selling is a team, not just an individual, activity.
4. An attitude that the institution is special and worthy of a superior effort.
5. An attitude that management's commitment to a selling philosophy is real.
6. An attitude (on management's part) that existing personnel can and will sell under the proper conditions.

MAKING IT HAPPEN

That culture is collective attitude and behavior explains why it is so difficult to grab hold of. A wet bar of soap, though slippery, is at least solid. Culture is in the hearts and minds of each individual. This is why we made the point earlier that cultural change is as much destruction as it is creation. Building a sales culture requires rooting out contrary images, not just suggesting new ones. Make no mistake about it: Redirecting the hearts and minds of people who do not think of themselves as salespeople is tough.

Yet, our sample banks have made significant strides in changing employee attitudes toward selling and some of them, for all intents and purposes, have arrived. They have strong sales cultures; selling is in their bloodstream. We found healthy doses of *each* of the six sales culture characteristics in the banks with strong sales cultures. Not two or three of the characteristics, but all six. Building a sales culture in a bank may not be easy, but it can be done. From our research, we learned that it has been done.

The chapters to follow present, in sequence, the essential steps in building a sales culture. Each element of the sales loop model is important to sales culture development. However, we can introduce at this juncture three critical *prerequisites* to sales culture development. Most banks will not come close to realizing their fullest potential as selling institutions unless they have these prerequisites.

Evolutionary Process

Developing a sales culture must be an *evolutionary process.* The attitudes and behavior of people need to be nurtured, shaped, helped along *over time.* Thomas Peters (1978) writes: "Most change occurs incrementally, and major change typically emerges over a long period of time." Redirecting an organization's culture represents "major change." It requires a determined, unwavering, systematic, yet evolutionary, process. Internal newness best comes in bite-sized pieces rather than all at once. Too much change at one time can be overwhelming and breed fear. The object of a sales culture is to *pave the way* for a sustainable sales program, one that keeps getting better. The experiences of our sample banks suggest that a sustainable selling program is more likely when change is introduced in human-size doses, when a climate of trying rather than a climate of fear prevails, when the larger pressure to sell comes from within, rather than from above.

The evolution point is especially important to communicate because many senior bank executives feel—appropriately so—a sense of urgency for getting on with the bank's sales program. Unfortunately, no *quick fixes* exist when the task at hand is building a sales culture and program. Attempts at quick-fix solutions only make it harder to build a real program at a later time. Bank executives need to couple their sense of urgency with a mind-set of evolution rather than revolution. As one bank executive put it: "you don't have to accomplish it all over-night. . . . Don't close on a Friday and open up Monday with a different company."

Sales Defender

Developing a new culture from an old one is an especially fragile undertaking. Resistance is inevitable. Not everyone will be willing to go along for the ride even under the best of conditions. Change is often uncomfortable. Some—perhaps most— will opt for comfort if given the choice. Some may go further and fight for comfort; they seek to destroy organizational newness to preserve the status quo.

A *sales defender* role needs to be played in many bank organizations as the sales culture evolves. The fragility of the process—the minefields seemingly everywhere—requires this role be played. Only a very senior executive, such as the CEO or president, can effectively assume this role. The role calls for the "clout" that only the most senior executives would possess. In every way, the sales defender must make it clear that selling behavior is expected, that "this is the way it's going to be." The sales defender will accomplish this only when actions back up words; words alone are not enough.

Sales Champion

Defending the evolution of a sales culture is vital. Just as vital, however, is putting into motion the steps that will cause it to occur. Someone in the organization must have the persistence, energy, vision, and credibility to plan, steer, coordinate, and nurse the process by which a sales program is implemented and refined. This person performs the *sales champion* role. The sales champion, frequently a director of marketing or sales coordinator—and necessarily high enough in the organization to be credible—must join forces with the sales defender to execute the most difficult sale of them all: the internal sale of selling.

Sales champions need persistence, because early successes in a sales program are hard to come by and it is easy to become discouraged. They need energy because "the task" is actually many tasks; at times the challenge will seem simply awesome. They need vision, because a sustainable sales program requires a master plan. Although the sales champion will roll the sales program out in stages, he or she should see the "big picture" from the start. This requires an analytical, conceptual approach; it requires "vision." Finally, sales champions need credibility so that organizational members will pay some attention. For this reason, it is especially risky to bring a non-banker into the bank to perform the sales champion role. Using an outsider may work, but the odds are against it. It helps immensely if the sales champion is a banker who understands the nuances of the bank's culture and the realities of running a busy branch or signing off on a multi-million dollar loan.

Different sales champions will likely be needed for major divisions of large institutions. Different sales defenders may be needed as well. In a community bank, the CEO may well play both the sales defender and sales champion roles. Who and how many people should be involved in these roles is institution-specific. One way or another, however, the roles need to be played. Teamwork among the sales defender(s) and sale champion(s) is essential. The route taken in one of the sample banks is instructive.

The marketing director developed the parameters of the sales program and then sold the president. The president *and* the marketing director then met with the head of trust, the head of lending, and so forth, to sell the concept. As the president said: "These were the key people—the functional heads—because most of the employees in the bank work for them. They have to stress sales."

CONCLUSION

Building a sales culture is part and parcel of the entire sales loop. Each of the other elements of the sales loop contributes to the development of a sales culture. And the existence of a sales culture supports all of the other elements. Culture is the key attitudes and behaviors of members of a group. It is what people think and what people do. A sales culture exists in a bank when these attitudes and behaviors are *pro-selling*. Selling is perceived as legitimate and important; most personnel in contact positions view selling as part of their job and are motivated to engage in selling behavior.

Most of the sample banks have sales cultures. The ones that don't are making progress towards sales cultures. We identified six characteristics of a sales culture. The banks with the strongest sales cultures had all six:

1. Customer orientation.
2. Pervasive selling attitude.
3. Sense of team.

4. Institutional pride.
5. Visible top management commitment.
6. Faith in employees.

We also identified three prerequisites for building a sales culture:

1. Evolutionary process.
2. Sales defender.
3. Sales champion.

Sales culture development is slippery stuff under the best of circumstances. Yet, it can be done and has been done—and in many more banks than just the ones in our study. We now turn, in the rest of the Sales Loop Model chapters, to a series of essential steps in *making it happen.*

5

Defining
the Sales Task

"You cannot expect a teller to
sell products unless you take all
of the activity away from her. If
you told our tellers they have to
give a sales pitch to every customer who walks up, you are going to have raving maniacs on
your hands."
A bank vice president.

Just what it is that contact personnel should do in the selling role—specific selling tasks—must be defined early in the process of building a sales program. Determining the desired selling behaviors and limiting them to the most essential ones helps salespeople to know what it is they are supposed to do, to focus their efforts on these tasks, and to have some benchmarks to gauge how they are doing. The importance of sales task definition is underscored clearly in research with industrial salesmen by Churchill, Ford, and Walker (1976) and in research with pharmaceutical salesmen by Futrell, Swan, and Todd (1976).

Churchill, *et al.* hypothesized that salesmen would experience lower overall job satisfaction the greater their degree of role ambiquity. Sales role ambiquity involved not having the necessary information to perform the job adequately, and having uncertainty concerning the expectations of role partners (such as other salespeople, supervisors, and customers), how to

■ The Sales Loop

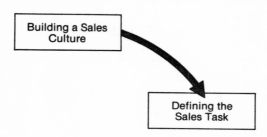

behave to satisfy those expectations, or how performance would be evaluated. Their results confirmed the hypothesis. They write: "As expected, the salesman who is uncertain about what is expected of him on the job, how to satisfy the expectations, and how his performance will be evaluated is more likely to be dissatisfied with the job itself than the salesman who does not feel such ambiquity."

Futrell, *et al.* hypothesized that a positive relationship existed between perceived sales goal clarity and sales task performance. The researchers measured perceived sales goal clarity by having salespeople respond to the following statements:

1. In my job I am often unclear as to how well I have done in the eyes of my superior.
2. In my job I am clear on the results expected by my superior.
3. In my job I am clear on the relative importance of the goals expected of me by my superior.

The findings showed that goal clarity was positively related to the salesperson's general attitude and willingness to work hard. The research team writes:

> This study's findings support the underlying theory of the management control process. According to this theory, job goals should be clearly established with the salesman; he should be made aware of their importance; he should be evaluated on his performance; and he should be furnished constant feedback on how well he is meeting the organization's expectations of him.

Our own findings support the conclusions from the research cited. The importance of precisely defined sales tasks became evident to us as the result of our visits to the sample banks. To illustrate, examples of just three of the practices we discovered follow:

The manager of the cash management division in one bank expected his salespeople to do three things: (1) call on prospects and convert them to customers; (2) retain existing business through frequent follow-up calls; and (3) achieve an overall monthly sales volume goal. As he said in the interview: "You don't need 18 goals. We give them a few."

The manager of a regional group of calling officers said: "I never have more than four to six goals in mind for a given person: numbers of accounts (relationships); deposits; loans outstanding; fee income; and where applicable, expense control and development of subordinates."

A bank CEO asks his customer service representatives to cross-sell bank services, use the customer's name, and provide courteous and helpful service to *all* customers. He has instituted specific systems to measure performance in each of these categories on a continuous basis. We detected absolutely no doubt on the part of customer service representatives in this bank about what sales behaviors were expected and valued by management. They knew what they were supposed to do, they knew they would be measured on how well they performed their tasks, and they seemed highly motivated to do them well.

A Tricky Process

The process of defining sale behaviors is tricky because it is possible to focus so much on one dimension that salespeople become rigid and inflexible. This occurred with one of our sample banks during an early period in the development of its sales program. The bank stressed cross-selling to such an extent that customer service suffered. As an executive with this bank put it: "We had cases where if customers only wanted one service, we wanted them to go to another branch." This bank has since added other dimensions to the sales task with better overall results. Most of the sample banks successfully avoided the pitfalls of both too few and too many dimensions in defining the sales task for various positions.

Tasks, Goals, and Measurement

Defining position-specific selling tasks, setting sales goals for the people in these positions, and measuring their performance are closely related, but distinct, concepts. The principal ongoing selling behaviors expected for each type of sales position must be identified and communicated. It is not enough to tell contact personnel to "sell." What does "selling" mean? Does it mean "filling the customer's order"? Is being friendly to the customer enough? Just what are the essential components of the selling task? What is it that management wants contact personnel to do?

Sales role ambiquity—and its attendant negative impact on job satisfaction and performance—can be expected until management takes concrete action to define and reinforce the critical selling tasks.

Sales goals are statements—usually quantitative in nature—concerning results to be achieved within specific sales task areas during a certain time span. Sales measurement is a process to determine the results salespeople actually achieve. It does little good to define for salespeople specific selling tasks but to set no goals and forego performance measurement in these task areas. The absence of a measurement system, in turn, means that the reward system will be arbitrary rather than performance based. Sales goals and measurement systems are discussed in detail in Chapter 10. We mention them at this point to differentiate tasks, goals, and measurement, and to underscore the essential link among them.

Motivation is likely to be greatest when selling behaviors are limited in number, specific in nature, and well understood; when selling goals are clearcut, precise, measurable, and within the control of the salesperson; when sales performance measurement is timely, accurate, and consistent with defined selling behaviors and goals; and when rewards for selling are based on performance within the defined task areas (see Doyle and Shapiro, 1980; and Shapiro and Doyle, 1981).

Importance to Sales Coordinator

Thus far we have emphasized the importance of sales task definition from the viewpoint of the salesperson. But defining the sales task is also a critical step from the viewpoint of those responsible for planning and coordinating a sales program. The reality is that it is virtually impossible to put together the components of a solid sales program absent precise definitions of selling tasks. Coordinators cannot know what qualifications and characteristics to suggest to those interviewing candidates for selling positions without first knowing what people in these positions are supposed to do. Effective sales aids cannot be developed without a clear understanding of the types of sales behaviors to be achieved. Sales skills training must emphasize the important sales behaviors if personnel are to have the competence and confidence to engage in these behaviors. And, as noted, sales goals, sales measurement, and sales rewards need to be linked to defined selling tasks. Clearly, sales task definition is not only an essential step, but an essential early step. Hence its placement as the second element in the nine-element Sales Loop Model.

GUIDELINES FOR DEFINING SALES TASKS

Defining sales tasks is a formal step. Banks that have yet to take this step may wish to pull together a high-level, interdepartmental task force to develop—and commit to paper—sales task definitions for each type of contact position. This is not as easy to do as one might assume.

Thinking through what contact personnel—tellers, customer service representatives, branch managers, commercial calling officers, trust officers, board directors, and others—should focus on in their selling efforts requires confronting fundamental issues that go to the heart of the entire sales program: Why is selling important in this bank? What do we mean when we use the term "selling"? Which positions are sales positions and which are not? For each sales position, what behaviors are most important? What tradeoffs of non-selling duties are we willing to make to free up people to sell? The tradeoffs issue is especially important given the tendency in banking to load selling expectations on top of non- selling expectations in a given position rather than stripping away the non-selling activities. The point was made by a middle manager from a sample bank this way:

> We are asking people to be so many things compared to, say, the life insurance industry where the insurance agent sells. He is the most important person in the organization. Our customer service representatives have to type letters, assist in audits, balance customer's checkbooks. You name it, they do it.

A key step remains even after a task force commits its sales task definitions to paper, solicits feedback, refines its work, and obtains top management support. This step involves revising job descriptions to emphasize the specific selling behaviors identified as essential. The "task" of sales task definition is unfinished until job descriptions accurately reflect the key selling behaviors expected and this information is communicated to the parties affected. Table 5–1, "Examples of Sales Task Definitions," illustrates the concept of sales task definition for three customer contact positions: tellers, new accounts representatives, and calling officers. The behaviors listed are meant only to illustrate the concept. Note that the sample behaviors concern "what to do" rather than "how to do it." Sales task definition should focus on outcomes rather than methods.

CONCLUSION

Defining the sales task for each sales position in a bank provides points of focus and emphasis for personnel in these positions. Management can hardly expect sales personnel to know what is expected if management itself has not yet figured it out.

Sales task definition is a critical, early step in developing a sales program. Salesperson motivation depends on a strong linkage among sales tasks, sales goals, sales measurement, and sales rewards. Design of sales skills training, development of sales aids, and other elements of a full-fledged sales program are similarly dependent upon clear definition of the sales task.

TABLE 5-1 ■ Examples of Sales Task Definitions ████████████

Position	Selling Behaviors Expected
Teller	1. Give a pleasant greeting to each customer.
	2. Perform "clue" selling and refer customers to the new accounts desk.
	3. Thank the customer by name.
New accounts representative	1. Determine the nature and extent of each customer's financial service needs.
	2. Make the customer aware of the benefits of at least one service in addition to the one the customer requests.
	3. Give each customer the best possible service, regardless of the size of the account being opened, the customer's appearance, etc.
	4. Thank the customer by name.
Calling officer	1. Call on every assigned account at least once per year.
	2. Present a need-meeting bank service to every assigned account at least once per year.
	3 Make at least 25% of each year's total calls on non-customer prospects.
	4. Cross-sell a full range of financial services.

Defining the sales task is a formal step. Definitions must be committed to paper, incorporated into job descriptions, and communicated. Thinking through what selling should mean for a given position in a given bank is an important enough process to warrant the considerable amount of time and energy that will be required to do it right.

6

Having the
Right People to Sell

"If you, Mr. Banker, owned 51%
of your organization, would you
follow your present personnel
policies and practices?"
A commercial loan sales manager.

Given the banking industry's present state, as indicated by our Phase I results, we were uncertain as to the type of salespeople we would find in our bank visits. Yet we will always remember our first bank visit. We can still vividly remember after our second focus group meeting, one of us saying: "These are real salespeople. I don't see any differences between these people and the salespeople IBM, Xerox, or P & G hires."

In our other bank visits we found the same thing. Across America, from retail customer sales representatives to highly paid commercial lenders, we found people who loved to sell, liked the challenge, and had a strong need to achieve.

WHAT DID BANKS FEEL ABOUT SALES?

To set the stage for a discussion of "getting the right person in the right sales job," it is necessary to understand what the banks in our sample expected out of their people. We found that these expectations were formally set forth in the banks' job analyses, job descriptions, and job specifications. These documents helped to clarify the specific roles and activities they

■ **The Sales Loop**

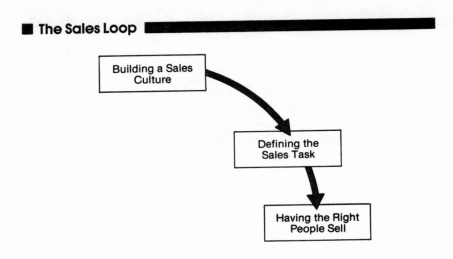

were responsible for. The word *sales* was highly visible. Employees in sales positions were expected to bring in a deal, to cross-sell, and to ask for the business—just like what Merrill-Lynch expects of their salespeople.

To see what the sample banks want from their people, let's look at what two vice presidents said about what they expect of their salespeople, what salespeople feel they are expected to do in their jobs, and comments from a sales manager of a commercial banking group.

The View from the Top

Top management's philosophy on sales can be illustrated by the following comments of an executive vice-president of retail operations. He said:

> We simply can't have the investment we have and not have productive people at the desks. We can't afford them at their "desks" and not selling. Commercial banking had a franchise on money, and it's eroded. The one institution people want to do business with is banks. There's only so many pieces of business in our market. We must begin reclaiming our franchise—taking money from the Merrill-Lynches, etc. How do we get it back?

Through selling. We are involved in a zero-sum game. When our sales go up, it takes business from someone else. Our people must be hired and trained to sell.

Another bank vice-president gave an example of how his bank is organizing to sell and indicated what salespeople will be expected to do. We asked him, "What kind of things occurred when you *really* switched over into a sales organization?" He responded by saying:

The biggest change is that 80 percent of the people in our branches were involved in some type of operations job. Today, maybe 50 percent are in operations; 50 percent, in some customer contact—sales—position. By 1989, we're predicting that 80 percent of our people will be in some kind of sales position and 20 percent in operations. If you have 20 people in the branch, you'd have 4 in operations (the manager would be one); of the 16 remaining—6 would be clerks and 10 salespeople. Four of these salespeople would be sophisticated and well-trained. They would be "super" salespeople who receive specialized training in order to serve our various important market segments. For example, one might be in real estate or insurance or financial planning. We are gearing up to have 80 percent of the people in our branches selling.

These two examples help to illustrate that: (1) top-level managers in our sample banks expect people to sell and most people hired at their banks must be willing to sell; and (2) these banks are gearing up to become even more sales-oriented. This will require highly trained, specialized salespeople in addition to the salespeople they have now. The people in the branches and unit will no longer "sit and serve" the customers; they will aggressively seek business.

On the Retail Side

To determine what was expected of customer contact people, we interviewed salespeople in every sample bank, including customer service representatives, consumer loan people, and branch managers in the retail sample banks. What we found was that the retail contact personnel we interviewed were true salespeople—there was no doubt in our minds. For example, one customer service representative (CSR) said she learned that a widow in her apartment building had a large savings account with another bank. She made friends with the lady. One night the CSR was invited to the widow's apartment for dinner. Before she left, the widow said she'd switch banks.

Another CSR in the same bank told the story of how her branch was given a three-month quota to get 155 discount brokerage applications. "I called all of my customers," she reported. "Before I hung up I asked if they knew other people I could call. Two weeks before the contest was over, management asked everyone to recommit to a larger quota." We heard many stories like these.

Let us make an important point here: These CSR's thought this type of activity was a "natural" part of their job. Their banks provided a sales climate. Their attitude toward selling was much the same as the attitudes of salespeople in other industries.

In another bank, during the conversation we were having over lunch with four branch managers, one male, 30-year-old branch manager said: "The way our bank is moving, the days of starting at the very bottom with no education are over. If you're going to be able to move these people up the ladder into a manager-type position, then you're going to have to start with a more upscale person."

A female manager in her 50s jumped into the conversation and said: "The person is going to have to prove, above all else, he or she can produce; that's the key to the whole thing; they are going to have to produce." "Their performance affects our performance," said someone else. "If they don't produce, I may not get any incentive pay, and my career may be affected. I don't want that to happen." She added: "People need to be better educated; some college, maybe a college degree." Another said: "Thus we will have to be paid more; and upgrade the status of our positions, to get a college person. People need more maturity; it can no longer be the cute, little young thing. The job we're asking the people to do requires them to be bright. Yet a lot of people with a college education feel the CSR job is demeaning. They want something in management. We need a person willing to put in a good eight-hour day and willing to learn."

Here is a sampling of quotes from still another sample bank:

"I never had a bank that made you take a test before you can go to work. The test involves math, logic, personality (type A or type B). Everyone takes the test. This has been in effect for years." (CSR)

"I was interviewed six times before I was offered a position with this bank. And the interviews lasted two hours or more. I felt like I knew half the staff before I was hired." (CSR)

"Through monitoring we have found people who are *not* right for sales. Sometimes they will come to us and ask to get reassigned. Our system is designed to reward achievement, not to punish ineffectiveness." (President)

On the Wholesale Side

On the wholesale side, a vice president and a sales manager of a commercial banking group said:

In the last three years, the 25 salespeople in our group have added 400 new relationships. These are good assets, moved over to us due to our sales approach. Due to our standardized credit policy, we took loans from profitable companies. We took these relationships away from our competition. These relationships will mushroom, since these are growth companies. We continue to call day in and day out on a prospect waiting for something to happen with the relationship he has with the competition. When the window opens up only slightly, we are there.

This statement reminded us of companies, such as Burroughs, Xerox, and IBM, who continue to call on prospects day after day. They might regularly call on a high potential account for several years until they get the business. Banks, of course, can do the same thing, as the quotation from the commercial banking group vice president suggests.

We asked this same vice president: "What are the main reasons that your bank apparently has been more successful in building a sales program than most banks around the country?" He said: "We're professionals—this is the cornerstone of our success. We are almost a bank within a bank. We use professional bankers who are used to production. We have separated maintenance [of the account] from the developmental aspects of sales. Salespeople don't report to the credit side. This makes for a unified effort. They are hired, trained, administered by a sales manager. We have an 'incentive driven' sales group. People are paid accordingly."

We asked: "Interviewing—who does it?" He replied: "The sales manager does all of the initial interviewing. He asks the regional vice president to do the back-up interview. We let the team working with the person interview him."

We asked: "What do you look for in a salesperson?" The vice president replied: "He must be outgoing; look and talk like a banker; but, if you scratch the surface, underneath you have a salesperson. The prospect expects a banker, so he must appear like a banker, but he's not. He is aggressive without being abrasive."

This bank's division does not hire from college campuses. They hire experienced salespeople. They were the only group we found doing this. However, other divisions of this same bank go to college campuses or hire from within the bank.

We found banks recognizing a need to increase the quality of their people and to have people who can sell. Please remember, however, that these banks *already have* a strong sales culture and their people are selling. They are "fine tuning" their sales organization. One hears more and more today that bankers should be expected to sell. Most of the sample banks we studied have already jumped that barrier. They are doing it now!

WHO HIRES SALESPEOPLE?

The banks in our sample take the hiring process very seriously. Managers know that to have an above-average or outstanding sales force they have to hire people who have the capacities to succeed in sales.

In the banking industry as a whole, and in several of the sample banks in our study, the personnel department carries out the hiring process. In sales workshops we have conducted across the country, bankers frequently talked about the "warm bodies" personnel sends them—usually people hired for retail sales. It was distressing to the bankers who had to live with people who were not "sales types."

Ideally, salespeople should hire salespeople. Managers accountable for sales results should hire their own staff. If that is not possible, begin to work with the personnel department to develop a staffing process that will allow the creation of an "all star" sales team. Ask the head of the personnel department to meet routinely with sales managers throughout the bank. Get the personnel staff out into the branches.

We still remember a young man coming up to us at one of the workshops. He was head of the personnel department in his bank. His department hires for the bank. After being in his position for one year he decided to visit some of the branches. He discovered no one from the "home office" had been in the field for the past five years. He was struck by the excitement he created in the branches—just because someone from personnel wanted to ask them what kind of people they should hire.

We cannot over-emphasize the importance of having the right people to sell. In bank after bank, we saw the zeal to select quality people. Consider this analogy: A "60 watt" person has the capacity to generate relatively small amounts of light (productivity). When the "60 watter" is turned on—with training, rewards, and all the other motivational techniques we discuss in this book—he can reach only a limited level of productivity. A "200 watter," on the other hand, will excel if each element of the sales loop is properly applied. The "200 watter" has a natural advantage, for he brings to the job his above-average talents.

Remember, *input shapes output*. In our opinion, staffing the bank's sales force with the proper person is a very important ingredient in creating and maintaining an "all star" sales team. The remainder of this chapter presents guidelines for selecting the "200 watter."

GUIDELINES FOR STAFFING

There are ten steps in obtaining a successful sales staff. The series begins and ends with approval and support from the top. The steps are:

1. Getting approval from top management.
2. Developing a staffing plan.

3. Preparing the job analysis, description, and specification.
4. Profiling the successful candidate.
5. Developing a candidate pool.
6. Interviewing the qualified candidate.
7. Getting additional information about the candidate.
8. Evaluating the candidate and making a decision.
9. Reassigning when necessary.
10. Getting top management to discuss personnel philosophy regularly throughout the organization.

Step One: Getting Approval from Top Management

The first step in developing a sales force is getting approval or support from top management on the *sales* expectations of customer contact people. Banks need someone at the top to support sales personnel policies publicly and forcefully.

Step Two: Developing a Staffing Plan

The sales force staffing process originates from corporate, marketing, and sales force objectives. The two major elements of the process are: (1) manpower planning and (2) employment planning. Staffing begins with an examination of present sales force manpower and a forecast of overall sales force manpower needs, as illustrated in Figure 6–1 (Futrell, 1981). This is followed by determining various unit, region, division, and group manpower needs and budgets, and obtaining corporate approval. These elements compose the sales force manpower

FIGURE 6-1 ■ Sales Force Manpower Forecasting

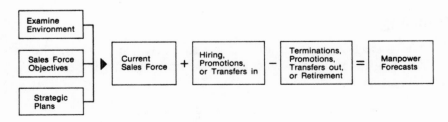

planning function. Sales force employment planning consists of recruitment, evaluation of applications, selection, and orientation of sales personnel.

As in any phase of sales management, it is important to plan ahead. How many positions will have to be filled in the next 6 to 12 months? Consideration should be given to additions to the staff caused by expansion, growth, new product lines, voluntary and involuntary terminations, transfers, and promotions. One bank in our sample prepares a schedule showing when additional salespeople are needed, as well as reductions in staff. It also starts the recruiting activity several months in advance of anticipated needs to allow time to find top people.

Step Three: Preparing the Job Analysis, Description, and Specification

The first task is to analyze the job thoroughly and objectively, as discussed in Chapter 5. The job analysis defines the position in terms of specific roles or activities to be performed and determines the personal qualifications that are suitable for the job. In many of the sample banks, the word *sales* is emphasized as a main requirement for customer contact positions and a minor part of noncontact personnel positions.

Job descriptions are formal, written statements describing the nature, requirements, and responsibilities (e.g. sales volume, territory, product line, customers, supervisory duties) of a specific sales position. They officially establish what the salesperson will do, and why these duties are to be carried out, as well as indicate the salary range appropriate for the position. The job description should leave no doubt the job is a "sales" job.

Job specifications convert job descriptions into the people qualifications (e.g. abilities, behavior, education, skills) the bank feels are necessary for successful performance of the job. Often, specifications for a position are determined by management in compliance with governmental regulations. These include qualifications for initial employment as well as the qualifications believed to be necessary to become a successful salesperson. Increasingly, however, statistical analyses are also used to assist in generating job specifications, as discussed in Step Four. By this means, the relation of successful sales performance to certain personal characteristics such as education, specific aptitudes, communication skills, personality type, and experience are statistically determined.

Guidelines for job descriptions and job specifications. Critics of job descriptions and job specifications point out that many are written so unclearly and ambiguously that they are of little actual use in the staffing process. However, banks can develop job descriptions and job specifications that they can use. The following list provides suggestions for clarifying job descriptions and specifications:

1. Decide upon job objectives and state them in the form of activities (what sales personnel actually do).
2. List the tasks required for desired performance.
3. Differentiate between routine and critical tasks.
4. List alternative methods of performing tasks.
5. Specify criteria used to determine whether the job has been performed successfully.
6. Specify favorable and unfavorable conditions for the attainment of objectives.
7. Specify other general information regarding the job (for example, title, salary, supervisor).
8. List work qualifications, education, and/or experience levels required.
9. Develop techniques for validating sales job analysis.

Step Four: Profiling the Successful Candidate

The next step is designed to answer the question, "Whom should I be looking for?" The persons to look for ideally should possess the outstanding characteristics of your most successful salespeople.

To identify potentially successful salespeople, establish the criteria for successful performance; that is, the standards by which performance is measured. It is not necessary to identify more than five or six key criteria. Extra weight should be given the factor(s) that have the greatest influence on sales success (Ivancevich and Glueck, 1983).

Once performance standards are established, the people who best meet them in your present sales force should be identified. These people in turn should be studied in order to identify the key characteristics that they have in common. For example, if all successful salespeople are between the ages of 25 and 30, have blue eyes, blond hair, have a college grade point average of above 3.0 on a 4 point system, and are lefthanded, one might conclude that only candidates with those characteristics should be hired. Of course, not all of the successful salespeople will have all of the same characteristics or to the same degree. However, if the number of salespeople a bank has is large enough, a pattern of certain dimensions common in successful salespeople may emerge. These become "success criteria," or predictors to look for in candidates for the sales position.

If the personnel department does the hiring of salespeople, various sales groups should provide the main input on the criteria for successful performance and information in developing the "profile." Remember, criteria and profiles may be different for different groups, e.g. consumer loans, commercial loans.

Personality characteristics. Many people have the mistaken idea that star performers in selling are born, not made. They have no doubts that individuals must "measure up" to the role of "super salesperson." Of course, this mythical star salesperson has a magical sales personality, has a sure-fire sales strategy, is a mental giant, is never discouraged, never fails, and always makes the sale. If they are honest with themselves, they know real-life individuals in sales, no matter how good, cannot possibly measure up to such a distorted, unrealistic profile. What does it take, then, to be successful in bank sales?

To get answers to that question, we asked our sample banks' salespeople what personality characteristics a salesperson should have. Their answers were the same ones research has shown to be important (Futrell, 1981). These 12 behavioral characteristics are:

Empathy: Ability to identify and understand the other person's situation.

Ego drive: The desire to make the sale, to be able to over-come rejection and continue calling on customers; persistence.

Motivation: Inner drive to do a good job for personal fulfillment. Achiever; seeks out new challenges and responsibilities. Must have needs he/she feels called upon to satisfy and a certain amount of inherent physiological and psychological drive. Goal-oriented, industrious, inspired. Likes selling.

Integrity: Honest, possesses social, ethical, and moral values, dependable.

Job interest: Demonstrates a genuine interest in "the business"; may have done investigative work as to what duties are required of a banker.

Interpersonal skills: Possesses skills in perceiving and reacting to the needs of others, meets others easily, likeable, friendly, sensitive, good listener, confident, sincere, open-minded.

Initiative: Originates new ideas and actions, self-starter, aggressive, go-getter, ability to make decisions, takes action, high energy level.

Intelligence: Ability to learn or understand from experience; able to acquire, retain, assimilate, and apply knowledge; able to deal with abstract ideas.

Communication skills: Ability to express one's self verbally and nonverbally in a convincing manner in both individual and group situations; persuasive, effective listener; presents ideas well.

Planning and organization: Ability to set up a course of action to accomplish specific goals, a good time manager, a planner, well-organized.

Adaptability: Capacity to cope with a changing environment.

Flexibility: Accepts new methods, open to change, can handle new and changing responsibilities, flexible, adaptable.

Though aptitude, personality, and physical traits are important factors to consider in hiring someone, they are not the only ones. Why? The bank can be fooled too many times relying solely on test results or outward appearances. Furthermore, if aptitude, personality, and physical traits cannot be related to job performance, the selection and promotion procedures may not hold up before a judge and jury.

One group of researchers analyzed 409 research studies that were published in 63 journals between 1918 and 1982. They found that, on the average, less than four percent of salespeople's performance was explained by any single predictor. They concluded that " 'enduring' personal characteristics of salespeople (e.g. aptitude, personal/physical traits) do have some relationship to performance, but not as much as characteristics that are 'influenceable' by sales managers (e.g. role perceptions, skills, and motivation). Who you recruit is important, but not as important as what you do to them after they are hired" (Ford and Walker, 1984).

This is why a single test, or group of tests, used as the sole predictor of success in sales cannot be developed. Tests are only as good as the people who use them. Doing away with tests, however, is like throwing the baby out with the bath water. Some banks have done away with tests because they feel that the Equal Employment Opportunity Commission (EEOC) is placing too many restraints on their use. However, the laws are aimed basically at only one end: "validity"—validity being the extent to which something is a good "predictor" of success in the sales job (Ivancevich, Donnelly, Gibson, 1983).

Success profile. One of the ways to develop a "success" profile for your sales force is to use a testing instrument that measures background, aptitudes, and personality traits relevant to the job. All members of the sales force are tested, and profiles are prepared of each salesperson. The test profiles are correlated to the performance evaluations, which have been sorted into three groups: success, marginal, and average. A normative or success pattern of mental aptitudes and personality dimensions is then established. Prospective sales candidates are then tested, and their profiles are compared to the success profile to aid in the hiring decision.

Step Five: Developing a Candidate Pool

The more qualified candidates interviewed for a position, the greater the chances of filling it with a superior individual. So, building a prospect list or pool maximizes chances for success.

Prospecting for people is an on-going process—not something one begins when a job opens up. Some of our sample banks' recruiters have developed a prospecting awareness—the ability to see prospects everywhere: on trains, planes, in restaurants, at conventions, shows, in social situations, in non-customer contact positions.

In addition to developing a prospecting awareness, the banks have built an environment that encourages people to want to work for their bank. Good products, attractive earning opportunities, a reputation for fairness and as a developer of people, and a well-designed training program are all important factors for attracting good people.

Many banks "work at" becoming the kind of bank people want to work for. When word gets out that the people who work for a bank are happy—because they are challenged, because they make money, because they are respected and treated like individuals, because they feel and act like winners—sales recruiting is much easier. Applicants will seek out such a bank. That is why many of our survey banks have people eagerly waiting to move into customer contact positions.

Step Six: Interviewing the Qualified Candidate

Many bank managers have allowed the personnel department to interview and hire their staff for so long that they are uncomfortable in the situation. Generally-agreed-upon reasons why effective hiring is difficult for some managers include:

- Managers lack interviewing skills. Often sales managers learn to interview by watching their bosses, who also learned from watching their bosses, and so on.
- Managers conducting interviews do not obtain information from applicants in all areas that are essential to good job performance. There is little agreement among sales managers working for the same bank concerning the characteristics they search for in an interview.
- Managers misinterpret applicant data.
- Managers' judgments are affected by bias and stereotypes. This can be either a bias for the applicant (Ivy League school, dark suit) or against the applicant (short stature, flashy clothes).

- Managers are susceptible to the "halo effect." If an applicant possesses some very favorable characteristics (is well-spoken, attractive), the manager may attribute other skills to the applicant as well.
- Managers allow the applicant to control the interview and are not able to collect sufficient information to make a reliable decision.
- Managers jump to decisions too early in the interview, failing to collect all of the information necessary to make a reliable decision.
- Managers actively seek negative information about the applicant, and depending on the importance of this information, they may also give it more weight.
- Managers' hiring decisions are affected by quota pressures. The number of job offers made will be greater when they are behind their hiring quotas.
- Managers do not evaluate applicants in a systematic manner (Futrell, 1981).

"The Interview Quadrant," Figure 6–2, helps to illustrate that it is not always easy to keep from hiring the "successful-looking" failure or rejecting the "unsuccessful-looking" success.

Indeed, we heard from the banks in our sample many stories of how someone who no one ever felt could sell was moved into a sales position and did an excellent job. Yet this is not an everyday occurrence. If bankers are unaccustomed to interviewing, they should ask personnel to furnish them with sug-

FIGURE 6-2 ■ The Interview Quadrant

Successful-Looking

	The Successful-Looking Failure	The Successful-Looking Success	
Performance Failure			Performance Success
	The Unsuccessful-Looking Failure	The Unsuccessful-Looking Success	

Unsuccessful-Looking

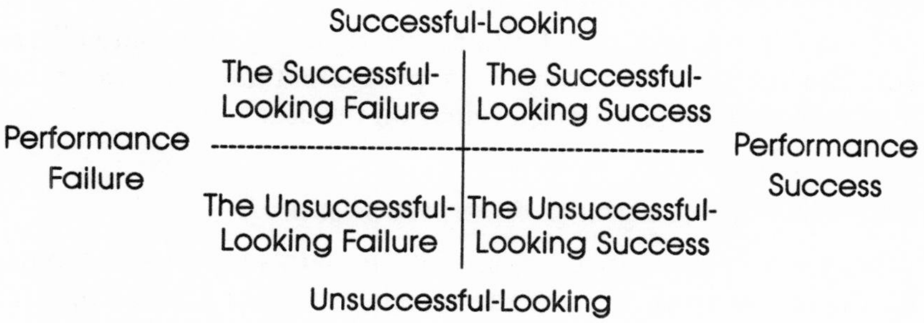

gested guidelines—including the legal aspects of the interview (Stewart and Cash, 1982).

Step Seven: Getting Additional Information about the Candidate

Checking references is a vital step that many interviewers fail to take. The time and effort put into contacting the applicant's former employers or manager within the bank will pay handsome dividends. One important interviewing premise is that *people tend to do in the future what they have done in the past.* We repeat both our successes and failures. Gathering the facts regarding a candidate's prior performance and behavior can be crucial in making an informed hiring decision.

Step Eight: Evaluating the Candidate and Making a Decision

Let's review what has occurred up to this point in the sales staff selection process. The candidate has been thoroughly interviewed, getting him or her to relate both personal and employment history. The candidate's perceived strengths and weaknesses have been evaluated against job requirements and success criteria. The candidate has been compared to other candidates. The candidate's references have been checked and the information given verified. Perhaps the candidate has been tested to get further objective information. Now it's decision time.

The ideal selection system is one which integrates all available avenues of information (including the interview, biographical information, references, and tests) to maximize the hits and minimize the misses. One should always keep in mind that any selection system consistently used in banks carries a certain amount of error. Rather than trying to eliminate all error, the bank should aim for a program that reduces error. That's the real objective of a selection process.

Step Nine: Reassigning When Necessary

Once the person is hired, many of the banks in our sample do all that is possible to make the salesperson successful. However, if salespeople do not produce or perform above average after a reasonable period of time—replace 'em. This could involve a non-sales assignment or termination. They must be reassigned quickly. The bank cannot afford to have low producing salespeople. The industry can no longer afford to "tenure" personnel.

In many industries, other than banking, a 20 percent annual sales force turnover is often viewed favorably. It provides fresh enthusiasm, improves sales, and increases the quality of the sales force at a lower cost to the company. Turnover can have a positive impact on the bank—if the low producers leave.

Step Ten: Getting Top Management to Discuss Personnel Philosophy Regularly throughout the Organization

Get your CEO, president, executive vice president to discuss personnel philosophy. Have them say repeatedly: "These are the kinds of people I want you to hire!" This is extremely important in developing and maintaining an "all- star" sales team.

CONCLUSION

Having the right people to sell is another essential step in building the sales loop. Enthusiastic, self-motivated individuals in the bank's salesforce provide the energy to make the sales effort work. They are the fuel for the bank's sales machine. Without these people the other steps toward building a full-fledged sales organization in the bank will be hindered. It is difficult to develop a productive and satisfied sales team with non-selling oriented people.

While essential, hiring the right people is also difficult. Good salespeople often do not fit selling stereotypes. They can be like diamonds in the rough.

Where possible, the hiring of salespeople in the bank should be conducted by those managing the sales effort. The hiring decision is too important and too expensive to be performed by someone removed from the selling environment. Sales managers should fight for the right to hire their own or to have major input into who is hired.

7

Having the
Right Services to Sell

"I feel good selling my bank's
product because I know it's a
good product."

A branch manager.

Products were "special" at the banks in our sample. We asked
everyone the question: "What are the main reasons that your
bank apparently has been more successful in building a sales
program than most banks around the country?" Everyone said:
"Our products." Yet when we analyzed all of our data, we found
that they were really talking about what we call their "product-
plus."

Before we discuss this new concept of product-plus, let's
look at a professor's (Stanton, 1984) definition of a product and
then relate it to our research findings. In a very narrow sense, a
product is a set of tangible and intangible attributes assembled
in an identifiable form. Each product carries a commonly understood descriptive (or generic) name, such as apples, steel,
baseball bats, CDs, or checking accounts. Product attributes ap-
pealing to consumer motivation or buying patterns play no part
in this narrow definition. A Sunbeam Shavemaster and a Philips Norelco are one and the same product—an electric shaver.
A checking account at one bank and a checking account at another are the same product.

A broader interpretation recognizes each brand as a separate product. In this sense a Sunbeam Shavemaster and a Philips

■ **The Sales Loop**

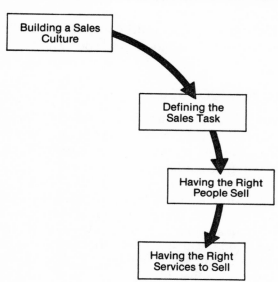

Norelco are two different products. Likewise, checking accounts at different banks are different, even though they are the same. The brand name suggests a product difference to the consumer, and this introduces the concept of consumer want-satisfaction into the definition.

An RCA television set bought in a discount store on a cash-and-carry basis is a different product from the identical model purchased in a department store. In the department store, the customer pays a higher price for the TV set but buys it on credit, has it delivered free of extra charge, and receives other store services. In this example, the concept of a "product" includes the *services* accompanying the sale—a definition that is valuable to salespeople.

Our definition is as follows: A product is a set of tangible and intangible attributes, including packaging, price, prestige, and services, which the buyer may accept as offering want-satisfaction. The key idea in this definition is that the consumers are buying more than a set of physical attributes. Fundamentally, they are buying want-satisfaction. People buy products not only for what they can do, but also for what they mean. Products, such as a bank's credit card, are psychological symbols of personal attributes, goals, and social patterns.

BANKS SELL PRODUCT-PLUS

What did we find at the banks in our survey? We found everyone in the banks, top to bottom, believing they were selling product-plus! The president of a community bank expressed the concept when he said:

> We have a historical commitment to delivering retail services. Our concept has been the emphasis on service to each customer; emphasis on quality service and quality staff. We have always concentrated on the quality of our staff. We give attention to the guy "at other end of scale," not just the upscale person. Our people are competitive, highly skilled, paid at the upper end of market. We have a feeling of pride. Our people are willing to go out and sell a service they believe in. They have pride in their bank and believe in their products.

A senior vice president of a multi-billion dollar bank said essentially the same thing when he explained: "We feel we are selling more than a product. We are selling a long-term relationship, starting with selling the bank—a respected, consistent institution in the marketplace. Integrity describes our people. We feel good about our bank, and we start with an edge because we feel this way."

With regard to new product development, the same senior vice president stated:

> We are the technological leader in our state; however, we won't rush a new product into the market until it is ready. We are recognized as a "state of the art" company. There is a certain confidence on the part of our market that we will be a technical leader. Our products are always good when they come out. All the internal homework is done before we sell a product. Thus, the employees have confidence in it. We are quality-oriented. We don't let competitors dictate our game plan in terms of marketing

products before we are ready. If you can remove a salesman's anxiety or wondering if the product is good, you really help him.

This senior vice president also detailed how his bank produces and delivers product-plus. He said:

We always tried to create value in product delivery based on issues other than just price. We never attempted to be the "K mart" of the banking business. The lender's job is more than renting money. The consultation role is very important, and this adds value and allows us to price based on total quality of service. We have a great delivery system. Good locations, good mix of locations in shopping centers, downtown areas. Our ATM network supplements this distribution system. Our decision to centralize operations centers allowed more sales space in branches. This also improved our quality of operational services. *Action Central* involves 40 people to handle customer inquiries on errors in statements, questions—all done over the telephone. This aided us with a degree of professionalism. The ATM program personalizes electronic delivery because the customer is the one who becomes the "financial wizard." The financial wizard symbol has a very high identity in the state.

Similar comments reflecting a broad interpretation of product came from each bank in our research.

Great Pride Is Present!

In the authors' part of the country, a hamburger chain has Mel Tillis in the ad saying, "This is not a hamburger; this is a 'Whataburger.' " The chain's name is Whataburger. It is clear that the ad projects an image of great pride in the product. In the banks we studied, the same pride was evident. For example, one bank doesn't have an ATM system; it has *THE ATM* system. It allows customers to become "financial wizards." Employees of the bank are very proud of this product.

In another bank we visited, it was plain to see it doesn't have an ordinary cash management account. It has *THE CASH MANAGEMENT ACCOUNT!* The facility is a beautiful 1700's style building with what must be 40-to-50 foot ceilings. It is on 100 Westminister Street, so the program is called the 100 Westminister Account. You cannot believe how proud of this product employees are.

Many examples of *product-plus* can be found in banks with successful sales programs. Let us give you just one more example. The sales coordinator in a bank said: "We're all proud of what we're doing. We are No. 1; we are the best. We are very proud of working for this great bank" (Note: She said "great" as did many of her salespeople). "We know we are a 'model' on cross-selling," she went on to say. The CSRs and branch managers in this bank talk the same way she does. Why? Because she is dedicated to the concept of product-plus and has *sold* them on it! This dedication to quality products, personnel, and performance standards are critical ingredients of a successful sales program.

HOW TO DEVELOP PRODUCT-PLUS

Enthusiasm for products can be created or maintained a number of ways. It's very important to have the bank's sales defenders and sales champions constantly publicizing your great products. Also, it is good to involve salespeople in product development. Even a bank with 25 product managers did this. And it helps to "tell" your salespeople you are involving them in product development because this helps to "sell" them on the products.

Sales managers should always have a positive attitude toward their products. This is very important. Too often salespeople feel they are selling products that cannot be differentiated from competitors' products. They feel forced to sell primarily on price. This can have a negative influence on morale if the bank's products are not the lowest priced in the market.

We believe that employee attitudes toward products can affect performance, absenteeism, gripes, and turnover. Should an employee's attitude create dissatisfaction toward the job, it could cause psychological withdrawal from the job, stress, anxiety, and even poor mental health (Futrell, 1981).

Management should also eliminate external barriers that may have an impact on salespeople's performance—a barrier being anything beyond the salesperson's control that literally prevents superior performance. Of course, what hampers one individual may not have a great deal of impact on another. Nevertheless, it can be useful to consider whether each of the bank's average performers is being hampered in selling its products by such things as:

• Inferior product quality compared to competition.
• Inferior delivery, product support, or other service.
• Noncompetitive pricing.
• Poor reputation in the marketplace.
• Excessive administrative load on the sales force.
• Arbitrary, noncompetitive policies of various sorts.
• Too many customers, too much geography to cover, or both.

As any manager well knows, these are common sources of salespeople's complaints. On the other hand, it is possible that salespeople may have a few legitimate excuses and, as Robert C. Townsend (1970) pointed out so lucidly in *Up the Organization*, one of management's key responsibilities is to remove excuses for failure.

Remember that the actual product "feature" (CD at 10%) may be the same or even less than the competition offers. However, product-plus also involves the bank's:

• Locations.
• Financial strengths.
• Physical facilities.
• Well-trained people.
• Reputation in the community.
• Quality service.

CONCLUSION

Product-plus is more than the standard description of a product's features. Product-plus is all the factors the bank provides in delivering, maintaining, and servicing clients' accounts. It is location, facilities, and people.

By providing unique combinations of product-plus features to clients, banks satisfy their financial needs better than any other financial institution. When bank employees are sold on the superiority of the bank's product-plus, they can become almost evangelical in their selling efforts.

Product-plus is a major part of successful sales programs. It builds pride, confidence, satisfaction, and sales.

8

Preparing People to Sell

"Projecting the image of know-ing what I am talking about is very important."

A calling officer.

Sales performance is affected by the capabilities individuals bring to the job, the capabilities they develop once in the job, and their motivation in performing the job. Preparing person-nel for selling responsibilities directly contributes to two of the three: capabilities development and motivation. Concerning motivation, preparation to sell is integral to self-confidence, and self-confidence is integral to motivation. Individuals sim-ply are not likely to feel motivated to do something they feel ill-prepared to do.

The costs of preparing people to sell may be burdensome to banks. But the costs of *not* taking this step are prohibitive: em-ployee turnover, employee ineffectiveness, poor customer ser-vice, lost business (Negri, 1973).

The importance of preparing people to sell was recognized by virtually all of the bank executives we interviewed. As three of them expressed it:

> "I view our limitation to grow is having enough trained cor-porate bankers with selling and product knowledge." (*bank chairman*)

■ **The Sales Loop**

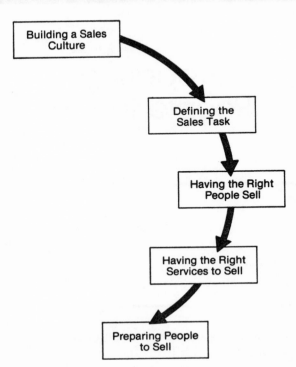

"We want our people to be the best trained. Competition would like to hire our people." (*sales coordinator*)

"The knowledgeable sales force is the most successful sales force." (*senior executive*)

SALES KNOWLEDGE AND SKILLS DEVELOPMENT

After conducting Phase II of our research, we came to believe the term *sales training* to be too limiting to apply to what banks must do to prepare people to sell. The word *training* applies to skills development, but not to knowledge development. This is a critical distinction, as sales knowledge development is just as vital to sales performance as sales skills development. The mandate to "*train the sales force*" is not incorrect; rather, it does not go far enough.

We believe the phrase *sales knowledge and skills develop-ment* (or SK/SD) best describes the task at hand. One banker in our study made the point this way: "We've gotten away from the word 'training.' . . . What we are trying to provide is the to-tal education process which allows the individual basically to go from preschool all the way up to graduate school. Eventually you could see this system going to levels of certification, tied to a level of expertise, tied to a level of education."

Our thinking about sales knowledge and skill development has been influenced by The Forum Corporation's research (1982) concerning the characteristics of high- and moderate-performing salespeople in six different industries. A principal conclusion of this research is that sales skills normally taught in the better training programs, such as probing, selling prod-uct features and benefits, and closing, have been mastered by both high and moderate performers. High performers, how-ever, go beyond these basic skills in terms of their overall knowledge.

Sales Knowledge Development

Sales knowledge development consists of four key elements:

1. Product knowledge.
2. The sales role.
3. Customer analysis.
4. Competitive and environmental analysis.

Product knowledge. Product knowledge is the founda-tion—the bedrock—of sales knowledge development. Sales per-sonnel need in-depth understanding of the features and bene-fits of the services they are asked to sell. They cannot sell a service if they do not understand its features; they won't want to if they don't understand its benefits.

The proliferation of financial services as a result of deregu-lation has made the product knowledge challenge more impos-ing. As one branch coordinator told us: "We have too many pro-ducts. There is not enough time for them to ferment before they come out with something else." True enough! But an outpour-ing of new products does not make poor product knowledge any more tolerable to the prospect *or* the salesperson. Sales-people need to know the products! Anything less is not enough.

The following quotations—all from salespeople we interviewed—convey the importance of product knowledge:

- "If you don't know the services, you can't sell them."
- "I want my customer to know that I know what I'm talking about."
- "We're cheating the customer if we don't know what we're talking about."
- "I've got to know what I'm selling. I'd better know lending. I'd better know the customer. I'd better have credibility."
- "Projecting the image of knowing what I'm talking about is very important."

Sales role. Bankers also need to understand the sales role. Selling is unfamiliar to many bankers, as we noted earlier. Its lack of familiarity encourages discomforting images: hucksterism, canned spiels, hard selling, half-truths. We believe it is essential in banking to break down these images while presenting and reinforcing the role of a professional salesperson, which is serving the customer.

Professional salespeople in a bank assist customers in making better decisions about their financial affairs than they might make on their own. Professional salespeople listen, teach, clarify, consult, and package. They identify the services that *fit* the customer, the services that are *right* for the customer. They are the bank's employee, but they are the customer's *partner*. Sellers as partners is a role with which bankers can identify. Sellers as exploiters is not. Incorporating into sales knowledge development programming the true nature of professional selling is important in any industry; it is critical in banking.

Customer analysis. Salespeople need to be knowledgeable about the market segments to which they will be selling. Demographic and institutional profiles. Services used. Undermet needs. Attitudes concerning banks. Attitudes concerning *the bank*. Attitudes concerning non-bank financial institutions. Trends and changes over time. Anticipated changes.

Market research findings should be shared with salespeople. Building market research findings into sales knowledge development programs is one of the most valuable—and least utilized—applications of this information.

Competitive and environmental analysis. Salespeople are "boundary spanners." They are in the middle—between the customer and the institution. In the financial services industry revolution today, the rules of the game and the players are changing dramatically. The environment is more complex and more confusing to banker and bank customer alike. It is especially important, given these conditions, that bank salespeople understand the "big picture" of competitive, social, economic, technological, and legislative/regulatory forces making an impact on the financial services business. Credibility and effectiveness with the customer are jeopardized to the extent that salespeople do not have this knowledge.

Sales Skills Development

Though we chose not to use the phrase *sales training* in the Sales Loop Model, that does not mean sales training is unimportant. On the contrary, it is very important. It is one-half of the sales knowledge and skills development equation. Both parts of the equation are essential. Both must be present. To give salespeople product knowledge but not the skills to transmit it to prospects and customers makes little sense. Sales knowledge without sales skills will mean far fewer sales than sales knowledge coupled with sales skills.

Sales skill development, or sales training, involves three key elements:

1. Persuasive communications.
2. Selling to prospects.
3. Managing account relationships.

Although these categories are not mutually exclusive, it is useful to think of sales skills training in terms of a communications component, a new prospect component, and an existing customer component.

Persuasive communications. Salespeople need not be "smooth talkers" to be effective. But they should be sensitive to those factors that can enhance the persuasiveness of their message, including: questioning, listening, empathy, organization, simplicity, body language, visual aids, enthusiasm, message personalization, and believability. Most bank sales training programs could profitably devote more attention to many of these areas. For example, few banks offer formal listening skills training. This is so, even though listening skills may be the single most important of all the sales skill areas. The best salespeople "hear needs." Or as one sales coordinator in our study put it: "The most important thing we tell our people is to listen to what the customers say and assume nothing."

Selling to prospects. The sales skills critical in converting prospects to customers are in certain respects different from those required to retain and improve existing relationships. Identifying prospects, call planning, making the approach, making a strong first impression, probing, and following up are key "selling-to-prospect" skills. With new prospects especially, salespeople must sell themselves, not just the bank's services. As a wholesale bank training coordinator said to us: "Eighty percent of the customers deal with bankers, not banks."

Managing account relationships. Keeping customers— and making them better ones—is a mark of exceptional salespeople. They view selling as *having* customers, not just attracting new ones. Accordingly, sales skills training should incorporate skills specific to existing-customer selling, including needs monitoring, staying-in-touch, and reselling skills.

GUIDELINES FOR DEVELOPING AN SK/SD PROGRAM

Sales knowledge and skills development is a "high stakes" endeavor. The costs of a poor program are more than wasted time and money; they also include ineffectiveness. A number of the sample banks had outstanding SK/SD programs. We learned a great deal from studying them. What follows are guidelines for developing or reviving a sales knowledge and skills development program.

Do Needs Assessments

Think of an SK/SD program as a product and, just as with other products, design it to fulfill actual needs. Base the design (and redesign) of a program on such inputs as:

- Surveys of contact personnel that identify the knowledge/skills areas in which they would most like to improve and that gauge their understanding of the bank's mission, its strategic direction, and the sales role.
- Product knowledge tests that indicate the product categories in which salespeople most need assistance.
- Shopping studies that assess employee on-the-job sales skills and attitudes.

These data taken together serve two functions. First, they reveal existing knowledge and skills weaknesses that need to be addressed in the program. Second, they provide benchmarks from which to assess progress once the program is underway. If data exist that show rising product knowledge or "shopper" scores, it is easier to justify continued funding for an SK/SD program than if no data exist at all. Data are proof, and proof is persuasive.

Evaluate the Program

Evaluation is closely related to needs assessments. Needs assessments concern the question, "What should we do?" Evaluation concerns "How did we do?" They are on different ends of the same spectrum, but both are necessary to maximize SK/SD effectiveness. Evaluation should be continuous and comprehensive—every session, every student, every instructor. It enables a bank to improve upon what has been done. A good evaluation program puts a bank in position to benefit from its experiences.

The sample banks doing the best job of program evaluation all used a *multi-stage* process. One bank asks program participants to complete an evaluation form immediately following a session. It then interviews the participants three months later.

Another bank follows a three-step procedure. First, participants evaluate the instructor and program on the last day of the session. Second, participants are interviewed two weeks later to see "if their manager allows them to use the skills they learned." Third, the managers are interviewed after 90 days to determine if program participants have demonstrated skills and productivity improvements.

Seek Goal Congruency

Sales knowledge and skills development programs should be evaluated on the extent to which they achieve specific, pre-established goals. These goals should be consistent with, and contribute to the realization of, the bank's overall sales and strategic marketing objectives. An SK/SD program is a necessary component of a bank's sales program, and the sales program is a necessary component of the bank's marketing program. Unfortunately, it is easy to lose sight of this simple reality and stress the wrong skills and knowledge in the SK/SD program.

If relationship banking is a key strategic objective of the bank, then relationship management skills should be stressed in SK/SD programming. If cross-selling to commercial accounts is important, then corporate calling officers need to acquire in-depth knowledge of non-credit services and cross-selling skills. If increasing the ratio of selling to non-selling time for contact personnel is a goal of the sales program, then it may make sense to add a time-management course to the SK/SD program.

One of the reasons "defining the sales task" comes before "preparing people to sell" in the Sales Loop Model is that SK/SD should emphasize the specific sales tasks salespeople are asked to perform. (Chapter 5 stressed the importance of salespeople understanding the sales task.) Knowing the sales task, however, is not enough. Salespeople must also have the skills to execute it. Sales task definition without the support of sales skills development is of limited value.

Think of SK/SD as a Process

Sales knowledge and skills development should be thought of as a process rather than as an event. To develop a two-or three-day SK/SD program for, say, customer service representatives and then to assume they are "trained" is a mistake to be avoided. The two- or three-day program is clearly better than nothing, but if there is no follow-up, no refresher sessions, no practice sessions, no opportunities to expand and upgrade knowledge and skills, then the hoped-for benefits are likely to be short-lived.

Salespeople, not unlike other professionals, need to continue to grow in their work. They risk staleness, declining competence, and lowered motivation to the extent that this is not the case. Indeed, ongoing sales knowledge and skills development is one of the very best ways to enhance the motivation and sharpen the abilities of experienced salespeople who may be getting restless.

The importance of treating sales knowledge and skills development as a process was clearly recognized by some of the bankers we interviewed. A bank CEO said: "People go through freshman, sophomore, junior, and senior years in their career. You need to cycle people back and give them some refresher training through this cycle." A branch manager commented: "Our customer service representatives are constantly in a training program on products as we are as managers. We are always attending seminars."

The best SK/SD programs are *never-ending*; they are based on the belief that knowledge and skills are fluid, rather than fixed, properties. One either moves forward or falls behind. These are the only alternatives.

Develop In-House Capability

Banks should develop at least some of their own SK/SD programming—even the smallest of banks. One reason is the need for a bank's SK/SD program to reflect it's own values and personality and, as already mentioned, selling and marketing objectives. It is difficult to achieve these ends totally when "canned" programs are the only ones used. Another reason is that in-house capability is more likely to result in ongoing programming. Holding off training until the consultant returns to the bank is unnecessary and wasteful.

We are not advocating that banks not use sales consultants. On the contrary, our research uncovered much evidence of the value of a sales consultant. The keys are to find the right one and to use this person in the right way. An effective consultant can help plan an SK/SD program, help launch it, instruct periodic workshops or classes, suggest evaluation approaches, prepare bank personnel to be sales instructors and coaches, or assist in other ways. Turning the entire SK/SD program over to a consultant, however, is likely to be a mistake. Preparing bank personnel to sell is too important for a bank to risk over-dependency, inflexibility, and stops and starts on the one hand, while not developing its own education/training expertise and resources on the other.

Stress a Mix of Approaches and Resources

The sample banks in our research used a rich mix of educational methods and resources to prepare people to sell; they did not rely on a single approach. Many of the approaches used are inexpensive. Some are ingenious. It is common, we found, to use people from throughout the bank as training resources (senior management, product managers, branch managers, training department personnel, senior salespeople) as well as outside consultants.

What follows are brief descriptions of some of the SK/SD methods and resources in use at one or more of the sample banks.

Classroom lectures and discussion. Sales knowledge and skills development went beyond the classroom in the sample banks, although classroom instruction was commonly used. As one line division manager put it: "We think you have to live selling, not just go into the classrooms and hear about it."

Weekly branch meetings. Once a week, at a set time, all employees of a branch meet for product briefings, sales skills training, or other educational purposes. These sessions are not necessarily led by the branch manager. Different members of the branch staff might be responsible for researching a product and leading a session on it. Headquarters personnel might lead sessions at other times.

Videotaped role-playing. Virtually all of the sample banks use one form or another of video-based training. Videotape offers visual impact to people who have grown up in a television world, allows the same material to be reused, and accommodates customization. The latter benefit is illustrated by the approach used in one sample bank. The sales coordinator videotapes bank employees role-playing troublesome sales situations that arise in the branch environment, e.g. the customer service representative is making a sales presentation to one customer and a waiting customer becomes impatient and interrupts. The taped vignettes are then played in training classes for purposes of discussion and resolution.

Using the product manual. Most banks have product manuals. The trick to achieving the best results is in how they are used. In one of the sample banks, sales trainees study the product manual prior to the beginning of formal classes. The manual includes service facts, features, benefits, and selling tips. The trainees take a product knowledge exam at the end of the first day of classes. On the second day, the trainees split up into teams of two to study a particular service, and then "sell" the service in front of the entire class. The trainees take a more detailed product exam at the end of the second day. In addition, each branch region holds monthly meetings for the purpose of studying a particular product in the manual. It is bank policy to have an up-to-date product manual in the possession of all tellers, customer service representatives, loan officers, and branch managers in the system. Keeping the manual updated is considered critical. The sales coordinator explains: "If the staff senses that the bank doesn't care about keeping the manual current, they will wonder why they should use it."

Mentoring and coaching. In the sample banks, a considerable amount of training occurs on a one-to-one basis. The approach might be systematic; for instance, teaming up an experienced salesperson with a brand new one for a limited period of time. We refer to this approach as "mentoring." An alternative is for sales coordinators or managers to "coach" salespeople individually on an ad-hoc basis. It may be that a particular salesperson is struggling in the sales role, or it may be a routine "check-up." Both approaches can be valuable. The first quote below illustrates mentoring, and the second, coaching:

> New officers are assigned "sponsors" for two months. Sponsors are officers already in the program. We use the top four or five officers in sales as sponsors. The new officer accompanies the sponsor on calls. In effect, the sponsor demonstrates all the steps; for example, how to select a call, how to obtain background information. Both people count the same call on their quotas. (*calling program coordinator*)
>
> The success of my job is having the ability to go out to the branch and be able to sit and listen to the CSR in her own environment. I like to watch her technique to decide if she is using the technique we have set forth, which is using the flip chart, being able to go smoothly from one product to the other, and not accepting "no" from the customer too easily. (*sales coordinator*)

Post-mortems. A division of one large sample bank holds elaborate post-mortems on pieces of business the division had pursued that were lost to the competition. The analyses include a historical review up to the loss of the account and the reasons the sale was lost.

Shopping the competition. Putting salespeople into the role of customer can be an "awakening" experience. This is the theory in one sample bank that devotes a considerable amount of time in a two-day branch sales course to the trainees "shopping" competitor contact personnel and then reporting on their experiences. The sales coordinator in this bank claims he frequently hears comments like: "Wow, I hope I don't treat my customers that way."

Publishing sales ideas. A quick and simple way to share selling ideas with a large number of people is through an internal newsletter. Several of the sample banks used this medium with seemingly good results. The newsletters we saw ranged from a simple one-pager containing sales tips for members of a specific bank division to elaborate, bankwide "house organs" that included sales-related material but was not entirely devoted to sales. These newsletters provided salespeople a means to share ideas with their peers, as well as an outlet for managers to communicate with salespeople.

Allow Freedom of Selling Style

Salespeople require the freedom to develop their own selling style, one that is comfortable and natural and plays to their strengths. Exposing salespeople to various selling approaches, techniques, and ideas is—as noted—very important. Allowing them room to use this input in their own way, however, is equally important. As human resources specialist, George Rieder, once put it in a speech: "Give me the game plan and the plays you think will work. I expect your leadership and ideas. But let me execute."

We think of this guideline as "the freedom factor"; it is tricky. A well-conceived sales script will help some salespeople—especially newer salespeople—in structuring their message and identifying key selling points. Where the rub occurs is insisting that the script be followed, or that certain procedures be used, or that a certain selling style be applied. Selling is tough enough without the salesperson feeling "straightjacketed." Some leeway for individuality must be allowed.

Our many interviews with salespeople and sales managers have convinced us that bank salespeople will be more confident and comfortable in the selling role—and will serve their customers better—if flexibility of thought and action is the rule rather than the exception. One manager we interviewed said: "People will achieve more than what you expect of them if you give them a fertile environment and freedom." Another manager stated: "We focus on motivating rather than telling people how to do the job. We have invested more on the motivational side than the procedural." A calling officer remarked: "There is no one style of selling. My colleague does it one way and I do it another way. There is more than one effective approach. Having a base of knowledge and hearing what people say to you—these are the constants. . . . A canned approach doesn't build relationships."

CONCLUSION

Sales results are a direct result of the capabilities individuals bring to a selling job, the capabilities they develop once in the job, and their motivation to perform the job. Preparing people to sell directly impacts two of the three: capabilities improvement and motivation.

We have learned in our research that the task of preparing people to sell is larger than sales training; rather, it involves sales knowledge development *and* sales skills development. Skill without knowledge and knowledge without skill are insufficient.

Among the guidelines to consider in developing or reviving a sales knowledge and skills development program are:

1. Basing the program on needs assessments.
2. Systematically evaluating the program.
3. Seeking congruency with broader sales and marketing objectives.
4. Thinking of education and training as an ongoing process rather than as a discrete event.
5. Developing in-house capability to deliver programming.
6. Stressing a mix of educational approaches and resources.
7. Allowing salespeople freedom of selling style.

Preparing people to sell is a "high-stakes" endeavor. To be ineffective with this element of the Sales Loop Model is to be ineffective in the entire sales program. Skill and knowledge deficiencies contribute to a lack of comfortableness and self-confidence in the sales role, which, in turn, adversely affects one's motivation to perform the role. The net results of these deficiencies: an ineffective sales force, poor customer service, and many lost sales opportunities.

The question is not whether or not to have an SK/SD program; there is no alternative. Rather, the question is: "How can we have a good one?" The purpose of this chapter was to provide some of the answers.

9

Facilitating Selling

> "The sales department isn't the only department in the bank; however, every department had better be the sales department."
>
> *A bank president.*

The best bank marketing departments are those that facilitate selling throughout the organization. One marketing vice president, whose bank has hundreds of branches containing thousands of salespeople, expressed this philosophy when he said:

> The sales force is the key to the overall marketing effort. We work for the support of our sales function, our executive vice president [who is referred to as the sales manager], and product management. We are a staff function supporting the line by providing them with advertising, direct response promotion, and research. Marketing is a part of the sales manager's budget. Our bank's sales manager works to meet his own profit plan, and we're a drain to their profits because our expenses are charged to them. If he doesn't want marketing's support, then he won't pay my salary because he won't pay our budget.

There are numerous ways bankers can help their people sell better, while at the same time motivating them to want to sell. In our research we found that facilitating selling involves four major areas: (1) organizational structure, (2) physical facilities, (3) technology, and (4) personal selling aids.

■ The Sales Loop

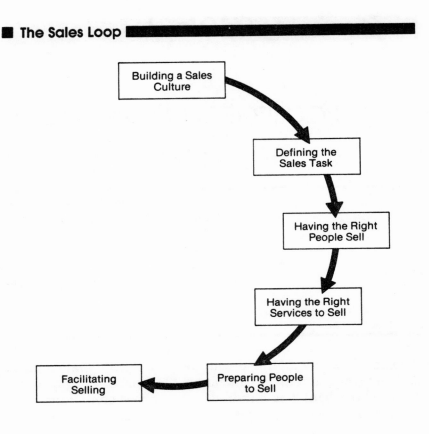

ORGANIZATIONAL STRUCTURE IS IMPORTANT

As we all know, organizations are constantly reorganizing, causing their structure to change frequently. However, with only one exception, our sample banks did not change their structures overnight when they converted to a sales organization.

We did not find one "best" way to organize the bank's sales force. Yet it was apparent that the design of the bank's organizational structure contributed to an effective working relationship between the sales force, marketing, and other groups in the organization. Paraphrasing Drucker: "The right structure does not guarantee results, but the wrong structure aborts results and smothers even the best-directed efforts."

FIGURE 9-1 ■ Relationship of Objectives, Roles, Markets, and Structure

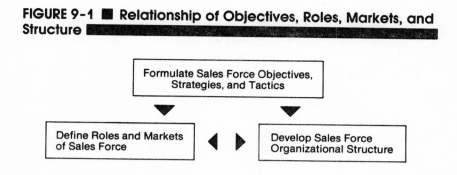

It is the highest level of management that is responsible for the design of an organization. Yet, because of many internal forces (e.g. management style, personnel, financial strength) and external forces (e.g. technology, competition, government regulations), management may not be able to design the organization exactly to their preferences.

Several of the main considerations in developing an organizational structure are shown in Figure 9–1, "Relationship of Objectives, Roles, Markets, and Structures." Short- and long-range sales objectives, strategies, and tactics are set based upon the roles and activities of salespeople and the markets they serve. The sales force organizational structure is then adapted to these objectives, roles, and markets.

A 24-hour change-over. Only one of the 10 banks we visited had made a major organizational structure change. The bank's top-level managers felt they needed to make the change quickly due to the intense competition in their market. It was a well-thought-out and planned change. The story is vividly described by the bank's personnel vice president:

> We went from an order-taking world to one of really getting out there and pushing and promoting products. . . . The interesting thing that occurred was that in this 24-hour period we wiped out a whole line division; we moved management around; we went from seven to six divisions right in the middle of a heavy consumer loans promotion and the organization didn't miss a lick. The activity didn't decline; the morale didn't go down.

People were so heavily involved in the loan program they didn't
have time to think about what just took place. We violated every
rule to the textbook approach on organizational change.

Within one week after this change occurred, our three top men
went on a traveling road show; hit 24 meetings talking to
management, right on down to middle management, to explain
what just occurred. So the attitude at the end of this one-week
period was . . . "Well that's not so bad."

At that same time we pulled the commercial loan activity out
of three of the divisions and centralized them into one. The other
two became transactional divisions—basically retail. They have
limited commercial loan activity. That's how we got from being a
bank to what we now like to call ourselves—a financial
institution.

Note that the foregoing comments talk about a structure
change, yet they also address the loan decision-making process. Numerous banks gave example after example of how their
organizational structure, and thus the delegation of authority,
allowed fast decisions on processing loans. They could have
either a decentralized or a centralized loan decision-making
process; it didn't make a difference. "Fast" was a main factor
that helped them sell loans.

We asked the banker quoted previously if management
faced any resistance to this organizational change. He said:

We had a culture where all of our line people (the divisional
administrators and the regional vice presidents) for a long time
had one of the executive vice presidents fronting for
management, making their decisions. These guys didn't have to
make a decision. What happened was this guy, Bill, [his name has
been disguised—their EVP or sales manager] said, "You're in
charge" to the people in the field. So the divisional administrators
went back to their RVPs and said "Bill said;" "Bill is pushing this
program"; "This is Bill's program." Therefore, you had the
resistance down below these people. Well, once Bill had his
hands around that, we had a couple of Jesus meetings with the
senior level of management and resolved the resistance issue.
Bill sent a very clear message out to the system, to the nonexempt
mainly, that said, "My God, there is a guy sitting down in that
head office that doesn't need committees to make decisions.
Within a matter of hours, he can decide what is right and what is
wrong."

We then had to teach our managers how to manage a system. It's amazing some of the basic management problems they are having trouble coping with today. They really never had to manage as an entrepreneur does when he makes major financial decisions. Today they are entrepreneurs.

This bank saw the need to adapt its organizational structure to the changing roles and its markets. A slow change would take too long. Its markets were too competitive. Management had to act fast.

A rapid, overnight organizational change such as this will not work for every institution. It is rare in the banking industry. Several bankers told us it could take two years or more for a bank to make such a change. Yet, a bank can change, or adjust, its organizational structure rapidly if absolutely necessary. However, we don't recommend a 24-hour change. A slower, more evolutionary change, as discussed in Chapter 4, will be indicated in most instances.

Retail structures. How one of the top retail banks we visited organized itself to sell is shown in Figure 9–2, "The Organizational Structure of a Top Retail Cross-Selling Bank." This structure has evolved over the past few years. As can be seen, corporate development, and thus marketing, is separate from branch administration or sales. Marketing facilitates the selling efforts.

This bank's retail salespeople are on a salary-plus-commission compensation program. Thus, they rely on the marketing information system group to track and report performance for individuals, branches, and the entire retail system.

To manage their people better and to allow for upward movement in the organization, high-performing branch managers were selected to act as "group branch manager." This person is responsible for five branches.

The CSR sales coordinator is actually the sales manager of all CSRs in the system. She is responsible for *all* training, as well as product testing; she is the person her CSRs call when they need a question answered. She conducts systemwide CSR meetings once a month at the bank's auditorium, in addition to meetings as needed on new products. She also visits the individual branches.

FIGURE 9-2 ■ The Organizational Structure of a Top Retail Cross-Selling Bank ▬▬▬▬▬▬▬▬▬

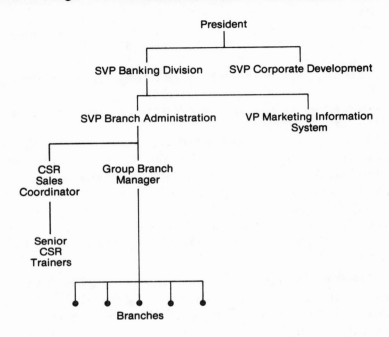

The sales coordinator has four senior CSR trainers who do the on-the-job training once initial training is completed. They sit at the new CSR's desk and coach her until "she is ready to be on her own."

Wholesale structure. We saw numerous banks with many separate wholesale divisions created, or being created, based upon specialized industries or "niches." Several banks are beginning to segment existing groups, such as separate commercial loan divisions based upon the size of the customer. Each division might have somewhat different management policies. For example, personnel in their small loan division are on a straight salary, whereas those in their large commercial loan division are on a straight commission.

Wholesale cross-selling. One of our sample banks is cross-selling on the wholesale side, driven by a bonus system that rewards one division when it acquires business for another division. The bank's various commercial divisions open up their files to other divisions. They feel if different groups within the bank are not cooperating with each other and supporting the activities and efforts of others, chances are the bank is losing a great deal of business. For this bank there are no boundaries between divisions.

The bank's "incentive" system is based on the premise that an employee benefits only to the proportional extent that the corporation benefits from incremental profits achieved through the efforts of the corporate sales force. Specifically, this involves:

- "A system of intracorporate credits wherein the benefitting department pays the selling department a "finder's fee" for revenue received as a result of the corporate sales force program."
- "A split of said credits with 60% going to the selling department and 40% to the employee."

From what we were told by many bankers across the country, many banks have little coordination and cooperation within their various units. As banks become more sales-oriented, we expect to see one unit within a bank helping another unit. This includes a retail group helping a wholesale group. If a commission system is required, so be it! It must be done in order to maximize sales and profits.

Design Characteristics to Consider

The organizational design and structure of a bank and of its sales force is based on many factors. However, the sales force organizational structure should be designed with the following points in mind: (1) to be market-oriented; (2) to be stable, yet flexible; (3) to be coordinated with other units of the firm; (4) to be organized around activities, not people; (5) to allow for effective delegation of authority; (6) and to develop a proper amount of specialization to serve customers.

PHYSICAL FACILITIES AID SELLING

Banks can also facilitate selling through physical facilities. An excellent example of how a bank can develop areas of the bank as sales tools was described in the March 1984 issue of *Bank Marketing* magazine (Barger, 1984). Hawkeye Bancorporation, Des Moines, designed each component of its Investor Center (IC) for a specific purpose. Located in the heaviest traffic area of the main lobby, the IC has an electronic message board and spotlights to attract attention of lobby traffic and to provide information. The daily rate board and menu board provide up-to-date information and suggest alternative opportunities. The literature rack provides information and helps to initiate consumer action. Privacy window walls support the customer's ego by allowing customers to be seen in the Investor Center but not heard. They also allow the IC representative to view the flow of lobby traffic and spot interested customers.

TECHNOLOGY HELPS SALESPEOPLE

Technology is a key capability banks are developing to help facilitate selling. Main frame and personal computers have long been used by banks' operations people. Recently, the computer has been employed to monitor the sales force. Tracking sales and supplying reports to salespeople and management are rapidly expanding uses of the computer.

Now banks are moving to help their salespeople better service and sell customers. One of the banks we visited is an industry leader in this area. The person in charge of computerizing its branch system in the next three years gave examples on the future use of the computer in that bank. He said:

> If the customer wants to know how much money he has, he'll just go to the lobby to an automated teller, punch numbers in, and, for a buck or two, can have a statement. We're going to have computers sitting in the lobby with terminals to tell customers if they can afford what they want. If the customer comes in to get a house loan or a car and wants to know if he can get it, he can punch [financial data] in the computer. For $5 he can buy a complete credit report and find out why or why not he got credit.

When the customer comes into a bank to open a new account, the CSR will input directly into a terminal. Once all information is inputted, you hit a button and a menu of items to sell appears on the terminal screen based upon this customer's profile. If you see he has a need but can't sell him, you input and send [the person's name and data] via *electronic mail* or some such method to the appropriate person who later contacts him.

For each service, we see banks developing a system so their salesperson can call up on the terminal screen the features, advantages, and benefits of the service, plus selling tips. Also, the salesperson can directly input numbers to provide the customer an instant statement on the future value of CDs, IRAs, Keoghs, or trust accounts.

In a few years, some banks' traveling salespeople will start the day by hooking a portable computer-printer-plotter combination into the motel-room telephone. While they shower, or have breakfast in bed, the computer will receive from the home office the newest sales leads that came in the day before, along with special messages put on the system by the sales manager—price changes or advice on how to counter a new competitive product that will appear that week. The printer will also churn out the leads the salesperson is scheduled to call on that day, including a profile of the prospect's product application, interfaces with the company, and buying potential. A recap of the salesperson's last visit and his comments, along with any problems the prospect may be having, will also be printed. The plotter will provide a map of the territory he will cover, with information on the location of each call, travel time, and an estimate of the time he should spend based upon each account's buying potential.

Computerized professionalism. Shortly, the computer will allow banks to move away from paper forms. This will reduce costs and increase cross-sell ratios throughout the bank. Bankers will have data banks at their finger tips—retail and wholesale customer, product, and competitive information.

When the new customer sits down with the salesperson, information will be collected allowing for a complete "financial checkup" and a suggested financial plan. The calling officer will do the same thing via a portable telephone computer in the customer's home or office. Complex financial information will be provided in a simple, straightforward format. This will allow even the semi-trained salesperson to service the customer properly. Emerging industry programs, such as in the personal banker, financial planning, and commercial loan areas, will find the computer to be their best selling aid. Numbers and graphics printed in colors and discussed in a professional manner will "hypnotize" the customer, making it much easier to tell and sell him.

PERSONAL SELLING AIDS ARE A MUST

The sample banks in our study made extensive use of personal selling aids. Many of the aids revolved around the *"Steps in the Selling Process,"* as shown in Table 9–1 (Futrell 1984). For example, it is necessary to ask questions of a prospect in order to match up properly product benefits to the customer's needs. For the CSRs of two banks in our study, the most powerful selling tool is the ability to open multiple accounts with a single—

TABLE 9-1 ■ Steps in the Selling Process

1. **Prospecting:** Locating and qualifying prospects.
2. **Preapproach:** Obtaining interview, determining sales call objective, developing customer profile, customer benefit program, and sales presentation strategies.
3. **Approach:** Meeting prospect and beginning customized sales presentation.
4. **Presentation:** Further uncovering needs, relating product benefits to needs using demonstration, dramatization, visuals, and proof statements.
5. **Trial Close:** Asking prospect's *opinion* during and after presentation.
6. **Objections:** Uncovering objections.
7. **Meet Objections:** Satisfactorily answering objections.
8. **Trial Close:** Asking prospect's *opinion* after overcoming each objection and immediately before the close.
9. **Close:** Bringing prospect to the logical conclusion to buy.
10. **Follow-up:** Servicing customer after the sale.

and simple—application form. One CSR said she could open six accounts in the time it used to take her to open one. By combining the single application, multiple account opening procedure with a *product flip chart* and training, executives at these two banks felt they had a *powerful human selling machine* sitting in their lobby.

Yet these were the only two banks using flip charts. One bank had used them and dropped them. Another said it was not going to use them. However, CSRs for the two banks using product flip charts really liked them. So did we.

Since one of the main jobs of marketing departments is to make it easier for people to sell, we saw them supplying selling aids that included:

- Comprehensive and up-to-date product manuals stressing product features, advantages, and benefits, along with selling tips.
- Prospecting assistance.
- A referral system.
- Sale brochures on the desk rather than just in a lobby rack so salespeople do not have to leave the desk and the customer to get them.
- Arranging for senior executives—including the CEO and president—to go out to sell with salespeople on that crucial call when the clout of top brass is needed.
- Sales call planning forms and procedures.
- A bank magazine for customers. One bank mails customers a beautiful magazine that spotlights a different aspect of the bank in each issue, plus business and social activities in the state.
- An internal newsletter. Many banks had such a publication, in which salespeople share ideas and selling tips. It also contains their sales performance data.

Today's salespeople must have selling aids more than ever before. These aids should allow them to "show" and "tell" their story in a simple manner. People retain approximately 10 percent of what they hear, but 50 percent of what they see. Consequently, there is five times the chance of making a lasting impression with an illustrated sales presentation rather than with words alone. Visuals help to:

- Increase retention.
- Reinforce the message.
- Reduce misunderstanding.
- Create a unique and lasting impression.
- Show professionalism.

Product changes and the many new products coming out make it difficult for salespeople to sell. Equipment and material must be provided to aid the selling effort.

CONCLUSION

Facilitating selling throughout the bank is a very important job. It involves designing your organizational structure so you have the proper delegation of authority, interaction between different sales groups, and key people to manage salespeople. The creation of physical facilities that aid salespeople in their sales work is also very important. The use of computer hardware and software to help the salesperson sell and to help in your sales management efforts is just beginning, but will be common in a few years. Finally, people must be provided the necessary personal selling equipment, materials, and knowledge that will allow them to sell.

Measuring
Selling Performance

"I want to know that others know how well I'm doing."

A customer sales representative.

Whenever people have asked us, "How did the banks in your study motivate their salespeople?," they are often surprised to learn that performance measurement and appraisal is a key ingredient. This reaction is not unusual, as most people feel that money is the main way to motivate salespeople. We found that our sample banks use a "motivational mix" of elements to motivate salespeople, as shown in Figure 10–1, "Sales Managers Motivational Mix," (Futrell, 1984).

Possibly the most important part of the sales loop is the major components of a performance measurement system.

REASONS FOR MEASURING SALES PERFORMANCE

In a very general sense, we found banks measuring and evaluating people's sales performance for evaluative, developmental, and motivational reasons. First, management could obtain an evaluative or judgmental appraisal of a salesperson's past performance. Second, this allowed the sales manager to make a developmental appraisal of each salesperson. The developmental appraisal is designed to help improve performance by developing action plans for future sales success.

■ The Sales Loop

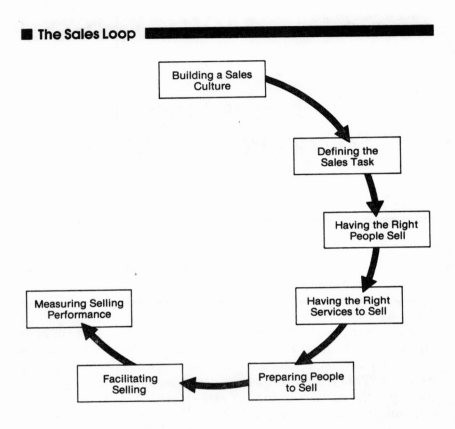

A comparison of these two types of appraisal is given in Table 10–1 "Comparison of Judgmental and Developmental Aspects of Performance Appraisal." Notice that the judgmental role is concerned with past performance and the developmental role with improving future performance.

These two reasons for measuring sales performance result in motivating the salesperson to improve performance. Motivation is the third, and most important, reason for establishing a measurement system.

The appraisal sessions allow the manager and salespeople to get to know each other better and to gain an understanding of what each person expects from the other. These sessions can

FIGURE 10-1 ■ Sales Managers' Motivation Mix ▬▬▬▬▬▬

Leadership Techniques	The Basic Compensation Plan	Special Financial Incentives
	The Motivation Mix Salesperson	
Performance Measurement System	Nonfinancial Rewards	

TABLE 10-1 ■ Comparison of Judgmental and Developmental Aspects of Performance Appraisal ▬▬▬▬▬▬

Comparison Factors	Judgmental Role	Developmental Role
Time horizon.	Past sales performance.	Future performance.
Objective.	Improve performance by rewarding based on performance.	Improve performance through self-learning, e.g. taking selling courses, self-study.
Method.	Use of evaluation forms.	MBO approach to goal setting, career planning.
Manager's role.	Evaluate performance.	Encourage and help salesperson.
Salesperson's role.	Explain past performance; react to evaluation.	Active involvement in developing future career and performance plans.

be a great help in developing and/or maintaining a bank's *sales culture*, if correctly conducted. A continued emphasis on performance soon begins formally and informally to tell people throughout the bank that management is serious about the sales program.

For people within the bank, this sustained concentration on setting goals and measuring, evaluating, and talking about performance gets sales and profit results. Good results. Results that everyone notices. This reinforces the sales program. People's attitudes begin to change about sales and their jobs. Many people start to come alive. Often, for the first time in their careers they are recognized for their contribution to the bank's success. They like it. It becomes intoxicating, causing them not only to work harder but to improve the quality of their work. They have a purpose for being at work. Bankers expressed the impact of recognition for their performance in several ways:

- "I now know that I can help my customers, my bank, and myself."
- "I didn't think I would like the program but I do."
- "I'm truly excited about working for my bank."
- "This is not the same place it was eight years ago. There was little to challenge me then. In fact, I almost got out of banking. Now, every day is a challenge. I have to produce to be rewarded and promoted. I like the new system. . . . I know that I'll be rewarded based upon my performance."

Who Should Evaluate Salespeople?

The primary evaluator of salespeople should be the salesperson's immediate superior because this person has direct knowledge of performance. The manager has actually worked with the salesperson. In some sample banks, the immediate superior completes the entire evaluation, including recommendations for pay raises and promotions. The evaluations and recommendations are sent to the manager's immediate superior for final approval.

WHAT MEASURING SYSTEM DID BANKS USE?

Most of the sample banks used, at least to some extent, the six-part system shown in Figure 10–2. We refer to this system as the "bank measurement system"; others may call it a management by objectives (MBO) program. One bank used the term "sales management cycle." Whatever its name, the process involves setting performance objectives, measuring and evaluating performance against those objectives, and acting upon the results. Typically, some groups of salespeople have their results publicized to everyone throughout the bank. After each sales period, the process begins again. Let's examine each of the six parts as to how and why banks employed this system.

FIGURE 10-2 ■ Bank Measurement System

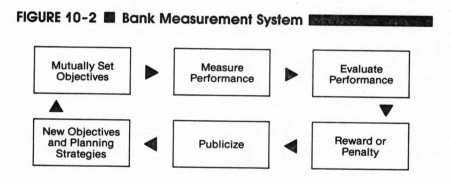

Mutually Setting Objectives

We were struck by the discovery of the willingness of several banks to mutually set performance objectives with their people. The personnel officer for a community bank reported that "our people often set their own goals a lot higher than we would set them." Another bank allows its branch managers to set their own goals. "We say what loan, deposit, expense, fee income, and income goals we want to meet," one branch manager said. "If we don't meet them, we have to explain why." Salespeople appeared motivated to reach their performance goals because they were allowed to be involved in the process.

One senior manager was asked why performance objectives are important. He said "because they provide targets, standards, control, and we can change our people's direction and behavior with objectives." Other bankers across the country made similar comments.

Objectives provide performance targets. Objectives give direction to individuals, the sales force, and the bank. Efforts and resources can be directed toward specific ends or targets designated as important by the bank—for example, a six percent sales increase on CDs or commercial loans. Targets, in turn, provide "incentives." Because the banks would reward the type and level of behavior needed to reach these objectives, salespeople typically found financial and nonfinancial rewards attached to the attainment of objectives. Job objectives represent the "expectations" of the manager regarding the activities that are to be accomplished and the level of accomplishment that should be targeted for the specified time period.

Objectives provide standards. Objectives provide standards or means of determining what job activities should be. They are a way to obtain feedback and to evaluate the salesperson's performance. Management compares the salesperson's assigned objectives to his or her actual accomplishments. Here, objectives become the primary basis for evaluating the performance of sales groups (i.e. departments, regions, districts, branches) and of individual salespeople. For example, sales objectives are used to evaluate the results of sales contests and to determine pay increases and promotions.

Objectives provide control. Because they serve to guide or direct the behavior of salespeople, objectives provide control. Control can serve as an indirect supervisory technique. The superior has the authority to require the full-time calling officer to average 10 calls a week, for example, and to send in call reports, so even though the superior is not working directly with the salesperson, the salesperson's activities are monitored indirectly. There may be objectives for total sales volume, individual product sales volume, or number of new accounts. The salesperson, therefore, concentrates effort on these activities (Berry and Williams, 1984).

Objectives provide change of direction. Objectives serve to redirect the activities of the salesperson. For example, a bank may emphasize only part of the product line during a sales period. Prior to the beginning of the period, sales meetings are held to present the products that will be emphasized to the customers. Sales objectives, contests, and selling techniques are discussed. If special incentives are involved, they are explained. Different behavior is achieved by placing sales objectives on different products.

Measurement of Performance

We asked middle and top management: "How would you suggest a bank begin a sales program?" Included in virtually everyone's answer was: "You have to formally measure performance." One vice president said: "We used to tell them to do this or that and did not follow up on it. It didn't work. Today, we determine each sales job's performance criteria (or objectives), measure them, and provide feedback. That works."

Banks in our sample developed their measurement systems by first examining the sales task definitions and job descriptions discussed in Chapters 5 and 6. Then they decided upon when to measure, guidelines to follow in creating specific criteria to measure, and what criteria should be measured.

Frequency of measurement. Banks measured their salespeople at the end of each performance cycle—a performance cycle being a time period related to specific product goals and/ or job activities. Several banks had concurrent monthly, quarterly, biannual, and annual performance cycles.

Several banks have their managers conduct informal meetings every six months to meet with salespeople on their monthly performance. They feel this is a great time for managers to see how they can help their salespeople. It also gives the employee a chance to "blow off steam" and release frustrations. Formal meetings are held at least once a year, with a written report on the past year's performance going to the employee and into his or her personnel file.

Performance criteria guidelines. For the bank's measurement system to be accepted by the sales force, and thus to obtain maximum results, performance criteria should be developed and measured considering the guidelines listed in Table 10–2, "Checklist for Setting Objectives." First, the objectives should be clear and concise, leaving no doubt in anyone's mind as to what is expected. They should also be measurable and attainable. If, for example, the objective is for the salesperson to improve his or her listening skills with clients, this is difficult to measure. On the other hand, a specific dollar sales increase is measurable, but whether it is realistic also should be considered. Sales objectives should be congruent with organizational, task, and personal goals. Finally, objectives should be developed for both the short-run (e.g. monthly, bimonthly, quarterly) and long-run (e.g. yearly).

Objectives can be developed that are both qualitative and quantitative. Examples of qualitative objectives would be encouraging salespeople to complete the local university's personal selling course or participating in community activities. Quantitative goals refer to specific sales volume quotas. Finally, objectives, and thus performance, must be directly related to the bank's reward system. A reward for attaining job objectives is a powerful motivational factor.

TABLE 10-2 ■ Checklist for Setting Objectives

Are the objectives clear and concise?
Are the objectives measurable for evaluation purposes?
Are the objectives attainable within the target period?
Are the objectives congruent with organizational, task, and personal goals?
Are the objectives acceptable to management and individual sales personnel?
Has there been a distinction made between short-run and long-run objectives?
Have both qualitative and quantitative objectives been considered?
Are the objectives directly related to rewards?

Quantitative performance criteria. Of the two categories of performance criteria, the quantitative criteria tend to be more effective in evaluating performance. This criteria category represents end results or bottom line objective data, such as:

- Sales volume.
  - Percentage of increase.
  - Market share.
  - Quotas obtained on individual products.
- Average sales call per day.
- New customers obtained.
- Cross-sell ratios.
- Gross or net profit on loans.
- Product knowledge test scores.
- Shopper ratings.

Qualitative performance criteria. Banks also used qualitative performance criteria because they represent the salesperson's major job activities and they help in the interpretation of quantitative results. For example, if a salesperson's cross-sell ratio is low, it may be due to ineffective sales skills. Care should be taken to minimize the evaluator's personal biases and subjectivity in evaluating qualitative performance criteria. Examples of such criteria include:

Sales Skills	*Personal Traits*
—Finding selling points.	—Attitude.
—Product knowledge without tests.	—Empathy.
—Listening skill.	—Human relations.
—Obtaining customer participation.	—Team spirit.
—Overcoming objections.	—Appearance.
—Closing the sale.	—Motivation.

One banker said "cross-sell ratios should be just one measure of performance. We use several pieces of data and other factors to evaluate our people." The "other" factors referred to were qualitative criteria. Many, many banks do this same thing.

Evaluation of Performance

The evaluation, and often personal interpretation, of measured results is a critical part of having a successful sales program. "It took us several years," said one banker, "to determine what to measure. We knew our people had to feel what was being measured truly reflected their peformance if our system was to work. Our biggest problem now is making sure our managers properly conduct the appraisal sessions."

This banker points out one of the questions all top managers have concerning performance appraisal: Do the sales managers properly conduct their one-on-one sessions with each of their salespeople?

Problems of mishandling evaluations. While the evaluation process may have its strong points, it can also backfire if not properly handled by the manager. A poorly conducted evaluation can create hard feelings between the manager and salesperson. It can even lower the salesperson's motivation level, job satisfaction, self-esteem, self-confidence, and other attitudes toward the job. It can take away future expectations of success. The result: The salesperson may reduce performance efforts or even quit the job.

Practical guidelines in conducting appraisals. It is important to conduct appraisals in an effective, professional manner. When beginning a sales program, banks found the following evaluation guidelines useful:

1. *Prepare for the inteview (both manager and salesperson).* The manager should collect all information on the performance of the salesperson. The manager should then contact the salesperson and establish the time and place for the evaluation. The salesperson should be asked to review his/her past performance, using the actual evaluation forms, and to review his/her job description. This takes place before the formal meeting. Objective data should be used when possible.

2. *Be positive.* It is extremely important that both manager and salesperson feel that the evaluation is a positive method of

helping the salesperson better do the job. The salesperson may feel he/she is required to defend rather than explain his/her past performance.

3. Conduct review with openness. Again the manager must be sincere and positive in discussing each performance criterion. There will be disagreements. People will tend to evaluate themselves better than their superior does. It is important to:

- Freely discuss each performance criterion.
- Ask the salesperson to discuss performance.
- Ask the salesperson to evaluate his/her own performance.
- The manager must provide his/her view of performance.
- Mutually agree on the level of performance that must be established.
- If there are disagreements, the manager should explain carefully why the salesperson will receive a low evaluation in a particular performance area. Frequently, serious differences of opinion occur because the salesperson did not fully understand what was expected.

4. Finalize evaluation properly. The manager should now review each performance area with the salesperson. Managers prefer to begin by reviewing the high ratings and work down. The salesperson should understand clearly what has been decided upon.

5. Summarize the total performance evaluation. The salesperson should be told how the manager views past performance. For example: "Susan, you have done above average this year. You are continuing to improve year after year and will receive a good raise. If you continue this level of performance, in a few more years you will be ready for a vice president's position."

6. Develop mutually agreed on objectives. Performance and career objectives can be established at this point. Both manager and salesperson provide input.

7. Formalize evaluation and objectives. Immediately after the evaluation session is over, the manager should write a letter to the salesperson restating the results of the performance evaluation and the objectives. A copy is sent to the manager's superior to go into the salesperson's permanent personnel file.

Reward or Penalty

Since the entire next chapter is devoted to this subject, it is not discussed here. However, note that several other important steps (setting objectives, measuring and evaluating performance) must be taken before a bank is ready to reward or penalize job performance.

Publicize Performance

Many of our sample banks publicized their salespeople's performance using a monthly newsletter, computer printouts, or both. We saw only retail results reported. One bank reported only the top 10 salespeople in its branch system, whereas another bank reported all of its CSRs' scores (e.g. cross-sell ratios or performance index). Table 10–3 is a hypothetical format ex-

TABLE 10-3 ■ CSR Report by Services Sold for January 19__ ■

Rank CSR Name	Branch Name	City Name	Customers Served	Sales	Cross-Sell Index
1. Sue Steenblock	Forney Ave.	Hearne	52	142	2.73
2. Kim Kimberly	Bryan St.	Terrell	56	140	2.50
3. Margaret Artz	N. College	Mesquite	56	133	2.38
4. Sue Jones	Five Points	Orange	46	109	2.37
5. Margaret Young	Main	Columbia	36	85	2.36
6. Judy Adams	Jackson	Center	36	83	2.31
7. Pat Russell	Main	Columbia	37	85	2.30
8. Cheryl Bunetta	Todd Ctr.	Wills Point	52	116	2.23
9. Joanne Blackburn	Oak Hills	Florence	39	86	2.21
10. Susan Helms	Forney Ave.	Hearne	39	79	2.03
:					
49. Sue Young	University	Cedar Hill	37	52	1.40
50. Amy Michelle	Oak Hills	Florence	50	70	1.40

ample of a common computer printout of salespeople's cross-sell ratios. Monthly newsletters contained top salespeople's photographs and statistics.

The publication of performance results captured everyone's attention throughout the bank. Salespeople worked hard to move up to higher positions in the ratings. In one branch we were told of tellers cheering when one of its CSR's ratings were posted and were the highest for the month. Branches were usually ranked in the same manner. Other publicized criteria were the type and number of products sold and their dollar volume by salespeople and branch (and even non-contact personnel's sales results in one bank) and the number of applications processed.

Many banks report only "news" items. The banks in our sample report sales results. They realize publicity motivates salespeople and tells everyone else that "selling is important in this bank." It reinforces their sales culture. "People do what is inspected rather than what is expected," said the person over branch administration in one bank. By the bank publicizing results, salespeople feel everyone in the bank sees their performance, so they work hard to pass inspection.

New Objectives and Planning Strategies

Now the process starts over. The extent to which a bank has effectively handled each of the parts of the measurement system may very well determine the success of its sales program. Take a brief look back at Figure 10–2. Within each of those blocks is a way to motivate salespeople. Put them together and they become a powerful mechanism that can guide a bank to success. So do it well. Formalize the process and keep it going in a continuous, positive manner.

CONCLUSION

We will always remember talking with a certain group of four branch managers. We asked the question, "What does the bank expect of you in terms of performance?" There was a long pause, then giggling broke out, and one manager blurted out: "Blood."

Another question we asked salespeople was: "Do you feel any specific pressure to perform?" Everyone said, "Yes." Their answers indicated they felt either individual or bank pressure and many times both types. A 50-year-old female branch manager of a bank expressed it best by saying: "I don't know if it's the pressure the bank puts on me or the pressure I put on myself. I don't know, but I cannot resist. If I think they have another dollar, I'm not going to let them get out of the door."

These are typical of many comments people gave in numerous banks. Performance was expected. Goals were set, measured, evaluated, rewarded, and reported.

Salespeople were very positive toward being "goal-directed." It was quite evident that a bank's measurement system helps people to become sales-oriented and performance-oriented, plus it helps create and maintain a sales culture. Many bank salespeople we interviewed were excited about the "culture" they were a part of. They were experiencing a challenging and rewarding job. There was excitement—even electricity—in the air. Selling was in their blood; it was a natural part of their job.

11

Rewarding
Selling Performance

Nothing that happens in an organization has a more telling impact on its culture than the behaviors that get rewarded. Senior bank executives wishing to build a sales culture in their organizations must be prepared to reward selling performance visibly, tangibly, and continually. One does not build a sales culture by giving the new accounts representative with a 1.4 cross-sell average the same merit raise as the representative with a 2.6 average. A sales program must have *teeth* for the players to

■ **The Sales Loop**

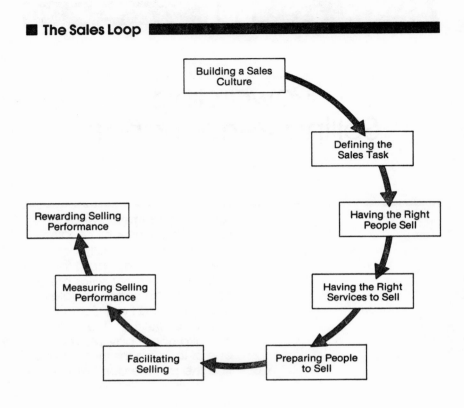

perceive it as legitimate! As the CEO from a sample bank put it: "You must put a price on what you want your people to do."

Properly constructed, sales reward systems will:

1. Motivate bank personnel to engage in appropriate selling behaviors.
2. Attract and retain qualified people for selling positions in the bank.
3. Enhance career satisfaction.
4. Provide direct performance feedback to salespeople.
5. Convey the importance of the selling role (Futrell, 1981).

Although all of the elements in the Sales Loop Model are essential, none is more critical than the design and implementation of an effective sales reward system. Behavior, after all, is shaped by its consequences. If certain behaviors lead to favorable consequences and other behaviors to neutral or adverse consequences, we will see the rewarded behaviors more and the other behaviors less. This is true for laboratory rats; and it is true for people.

Selling behavior for most bankers represents a big change because of tradition, stigma, and predisposition. Most bankers will take the "path of least resistance," call mostly on friends, and fail to ask for the business unless they have strong, compelling reasons to do otherwise. Without a sales reward system, most calling officers, for example, would *not*:

1. Be proactive in the selling role.
2. Prospect effectively.
3. Plan the call.
4. Use multiple closes.
5. Keep calling.
6. Call on hostile prospects.

Although a sales reward system is not the only means of motivating sales behavior, we believe it to be the most important means. To measure sales performance but not reward it severely limits a bank's potential in establishing a sales program; it is naive to expect selling behavior but be unwilling to reward it.

Developing an effective sales reward system is not easy. The relationship between sales performance and sales rewards is complex. For one thing, the bank has to determine which aspects of selling performance are to be rewarded. Many possibilities exist; for example, total sales volume, meeting sales goals, retention of business, account profitability, customer satisfaction levels, and administrative duties (Walker, Churchill, and Ford, 1977). Deciding *what* to reward is more involved than it first appears. Deciding *how* to reward sales performance is equally complex and we focus on that question in this chapter.

THE REWARD TRIANGLE

Sales performance can be rewarded in three fundamental ways. We believe a bank should use all three ways. It is helpful to think in terms of a "reward triangle" with three interrelated elements:

1. Direct financial rewards.
2. Career advancement.
3. Recognition.

Figure 11–1 visually presents this concept.

FIGURE 11-1 ■ The Reward Triangle

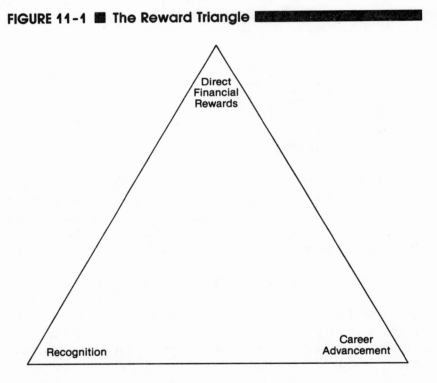

Direct Financial Rewards

Direct financial rewards involve paying more for better sales performance. The means of accomplishing this incude merit salary increases, periodic bonuses, sales commissions, sales contests, and other forms of financial incentives. Most of the sample banks used several of these tools in combination—an approach we encourage. Several of the banks did not reward sales behavior to the degree necessary, and this deficiency blunted the potential of other positive steps they had taken to develop their sales programs. The following quote from a marketing director illustrates the importance of "biting the bullet" on direct financial rewards for selling: "My next step is to do something about the reward system. We can't keep asking people to excel, to go beyond the call of duty, without compensating sales performance."

We recommend that financial rewards for selling be built into the regular performance appraisal/merit raise cycle *and* be supplemented in some other way. Using an individual's sales performance as a *central* criterion in assessing overall job performance and determining salary increases is critically important in building a sales culture. Sustained selling effectiveness is simply more likely when sales behavior is viewed as a normal part of the everyday job. Yet, semi-annual or annual merit salary increases, if they are the only incentive used, come too long after the sales behaviors they are designed to reward. The ideal system is one that motivates everyday selling behavior, offers timely performance feedback, and deepens the sales component of an organization's culture.

Sales contests. Sales contests can be a valuable tool to achieve specific marketing objectives and to stimulate added sales intensity and excitement during a specific period of time. Their best application, however, is as an *adjunct* to an ongoing financial reward system rather than as a replacement. One of the problems with a "contest-only" sales reward system is the tendency to overuse contests, diminishing their impact in the process.

We suggest that sales contests:

- Be infrequent (perhaps one or two a year).
- Last a short time (for example, four to six weeks).
- Have clear-cut objectives.
- Be easy to understand.
- Be fair.

- Encourage salespeople to act in the customer/prospect's best interests.
- Encourage teamwork (for example, competitions pitting branch against branch or sales region against sales region, not just individual against individual).

Commission systems. Well-conceived commission systems link sales performance and rewards in a direct and timely fashion and in doing so can provide otherwise reluctant bankers strong incentive to engage in selling behavior. The downside is that commission pay runs contrary to banking's cultural tradition and is still today regarded by many bankers as unprofessional and "unbankerly." That banks sell money that needs to be returned (with interest) aggravates the image problem associated with commission selling, since loans sold to the wrong customers can spell disaster. To be sure, a bank does not move quietly into a selling mode when it installs a commission system.

Four of the 10 sample banks used sales commission systems at the time of our research. All were clearly benefitting from doing so. A retail sample bank pays its customer service representatives a standard commission for each service they sell. Services are weighted in terms of the compensation they bring. The system is designed to encourage cross-selling. The bank moved from an average of about 1.6 services sold per customer prior to installing the incentive program to an average of about 3.4 services sold per customer in early 1984. Employees average about $60 a month in commission income, or about 6 percent of their base pay (Bennett, 1984). A branch manager in this bank said: "The bank was real skeptical when we started talking about incentives, but now it has been proven to work. The people who have been performing well perform even better." An executive at the same bank remarked: "We have a waiting list of people wanting to be customer service representatives because of the incentives."

A second sample bank achieved striking increases in middle market commercial loans through a system in which commission salespeople find borrowers, package loan deals, and obtain internal loan approvals then turn the customer over to a loan officer. Compensation is geared to a loan's profitability, encouraging the finding of creditworthy borrowers and sound pricing. One salesman in the program described his role this way: "We are the most pure salespeople in the bank. We book the business and then back out, with the loan officer replacing us as the primary contact. Our job is to bring bank and customer together." Commercial loans outstanding sold by this group increased more than 30 percent in 1983, a year in which commercial/industrial loans nationwide increased by only 3.2 percent.

The system is not without pitfalls, however. At the time of our research, cross-selling of non-credit services seemed to be falling through the cracks, the concept of one party selling the credit and another administering it seemed to work less well in large metropolitan areas, and some of the salespeople (highly paid and not necessarily bankers by background) did not feel part of the "mainstream" banking organization.

Bonuses. Bonuses can be a powerful incentive, especially if they are tied to sufficiently high standards to be achievable only through exemplary performance and are sizable enough to be worth the extra effort. And if the bonus program is linked to recognition for bonus awardees (a banquet in which the CEO hands out the bonus checks, for example), this is all the better.

Several sample banks have sales bonus programs in operation. In one bank, branch managers receive quarterly bonuses if they exceed sales goals set for their branches. These bonuses can total as much as 20 percent of a branch manager's annual salary for credit sales and as much as 40 percent of salary overall.

Key points to remember about financial rewards. Financially rewarding selling performance is essential in developing a first-rate sales program. The sample banks with the strongest sales programs *all* had financial reward systems in place. A key, we believe, is to build financial rewards for selling into the regular appraisal/merit salary raise process (and to make the sales/salary link quite clear) *and* to supplement salary increases with contests, commission pay, bonuses, or some combination of these tools. For example, a bank's management could develop a strong sales reward program by using sales performance as a central criterion in performance appraisals, instituting a quarterly bonus program, sponsoring an annual sales incentive contest, and effectively handling the career advancement and recognition elements of the reward triangle (to be discussed in the following pages).

Commission-based systems are an alternative but not a necessity. The sample banks with commission systems had strong sales programs but so did other sample banks that handled their sales reward systems differently. We wish to emphasize this point because bank managements sometimes reject paying for selling when, in fact, what they really object to is paying commissions. It is important to emphasize, therefore, that one can pay for selling—and do it effectively—and not pay commissions.

Some other points to keep in mind:

1. A successful sales reward system motivates salespeople to behave in a manner that meets the needs of the bank and the customer/prospect.

2. Reward systems should be stable. They need to be well thought out to avoid constant tinkering or changes (Futrell, 1981).

3. Reward systems should be performance-based. They need to be linked to the performance measurement system. Effective performance measurement is a prerequisite to an effective reward system.

4. It is possible to overpay with incentive income and in the process make salespeople so dependent on this income that they become insensitive to customer needs, ignore non-selling aspects of the job, or leave the bank during business downturns. The earlier example of the sample bank significantly increasing its new accounts desk cross-selling ratio with a commission system averaging about six percent of base pay is instructive.

5. The potential hazards associated with overpaying bank salespeople do not excuse the far more common problem of underpaying them. The old axiom that "you get what you pay for" tends to be true. As a sample bank CEO put it: "If you want above average people, you have to pay above average compensation."

6. Incentive systems linking performance and rewards are appropriate for all types of banking jobs, not just customer-contact jobs involving a sales role. The often-heard notion that it is unfair to non-contact personnel to institute an incentive program for contact personnel is a false issue. The overriding purpose of any reward system is to encourage employees to do what management wants them to do. Using incentives to encourage greater productivity among operations personnel is as practical and important as using them to encourage more selling behavior from contact personnel. When Union National Bank of Little Rock, Ark., instituted an incentive program for proof operators, these operators averaged 1,065 items per hour. Productivity climbed to 3,500 items per hour after the program had been underway for a while (Bennett, 1984).

Career Advancement

One of the surest ways to develop a sales culture in a bank is to use sales performance as a key factor in career advancement decisions. Management gives one signal when the best salespeople move ahead in the organization and another signal when they don't. Assuring that high-performing salespeople advance in their careers in the bank is perhaps the most visible statement management can make about its commitment to having a sales program. As one banker put it: "The types of role models that are rewarded with upward mobility is the most telling managerial support for an emphasis area you can have."

Making sure that the linkage between sales performance and career advancement is evident is vital. One of the sample banks is using successful participation in the calling program as a criterion in promotion decisions but has not done a good enough job communicating this tie-in within the organization. The following comments from different individuals in this bank illustrate the importance of making the sales/career advancement linkage clearcut:

"We were told special people would be taken care of; it hasn't happened." *(branch manager)*

"It's a slow, funny, working machine. The branch manager gets a bigger branch, has a wider salary range, gets recognized, and gets promoted." *(marketing director)*

"We have pushed our best sales performers along in their careers. I'm not sure we have made it clear to their peers why they have done so well." *(president)*

In contrast is the statement of a branch manager in another sample bank. He stated: "If I could not sell, I'd still be at one of the smallest branches." This individual perceives a career stake in selling; career advancement becomes an effective element in the reward triangle only to the extent that its relationship to sales performance is *perceived.*

Linking career advancement to selling performance is tricky, since a good salesperson will not necessarily be a good manager. Nor does a bank necessarily benefit itself by promoting an excellent salesperson out of a sales position. This issue proved troublesome in some of the sample banks. When asked what happens to the bank's most successful salespeople, one corporate banking manager said: "Unfortunately, they become sales managers. The institution is still geared to taking you out of the market and making you a manager rather than making it worthwhile for you to stay in selling."

An executive from another sample bank answered the same question this way: "The most successful salespeople, if they have management skills, are running our line divisions. Some of our best salespeople who were not good managers have left. A key opportunity is to improve the lot of good salespeople who are not management potential people."

Part of the answer lies in a dual-track system that provides promotion opportunity *within* selling positions, as well as *outside* these positions. One sample bank has designed three levels of responsibility into the customer service representative position, allowing CSRs promotion opportunities within these positions. The CSR I level is the entry-level position. Employees are eligible for promotion to the CSR II level if they have been on the job for at least one year, have achieved performance goals, and have passed a product knowledge test. The highest level is Senior CSR (CSR III), which requires excellent performance, passing a more difficult product knowledge test, and cross-training.

The manager of the cash management division in another bank explained his approach this way:

> If individuals have an interest in management, we commit to them that we will develop in them management skills. Most of the salespeople want to be managers. For others not wanting to be managers, we try to give them title, grade, and money. Salary is dependent upon job grade, and each sales job can be one of three grades. A person can move through all three of these grades. They can get promoted and stay a salesperson in the same territory.

Another part of the answer involves rethinking salary classification systems that "cap" salary potential after an individual has advanced several grades, in effect forcing some people out of positions for which they are best suited. As one experienced customer service representative said: "Why can't they reward my success with more money, rather than me having to change my job?"

Recognition

Financial and career benefits are both essential component parts of a sales reward system. Equally important is *recognition* of outstanding sales performance. Recognition can come in many forms; its powerfulness is related to the sincerity with which it is given, rather than the dollars and cents expended to provide it. One new accounts representative made the point particularly well: "It's not the size of the gift that counts; it's that they take the time to recognize you that counts."

Again and again in our research, we saw evidence of the profound motivational impact of recognition. Recognition can come from superiors, peers, even customers. The words of salespeople we interviewed illustrate each type:

> "When you get recognized for doing good, it makes you go for it." *(customer service representative)*

"If two or three people come up and say you had a great month, that gets the adrenaline flowing." (branch manager)

"I like recognition for myself. Is that a flaw in my personality?" (branch manager)

"My name is recognized, always up before senior management; the way people know me is via my sales results." (customer service representative)

"I enjoy having customers come back who want to talk with me." (customer service representative)

"We get Christmas cards from customers." (customer service representative)

The assumption that good salespeople are driven only by money is wrong. We asked every salesperson we interviewed this question: "What more than anything else motivates you to want to sell?" Only rarely was money first mentioned. Respondents mostly spoke of helping customers, achieving personal satisfaction, pride, and recognition. This finding is consistent with many studies that have concluded money is not the primary motivator of people at work (Herzberg, et al., 1959; Lawler, 1971).

Virtually all of the sample banks employed recognition programs. The least formal—and one of the most effective—was the practice of one CEO to send handwritten congratulatory notes to salespeople making a big sale or having a good sales period. Another bank has a "million dollar club" and a traveling award—a "strong box" trophy in a glass case—that goes to the most outstanding branch office. Another bank holds quarterly sales awards dinners presided over by the CEO or president. Still another bank has a "president's club," which involves a recognition dinner for top sales performers and spouses, a certificate of achievement, and gifts. Several banks regularly publish feature articles on top salespeople in their house organs.

It is difficult to overstate the significance of recognition programs. If viewed as a complement to the other elements in the reward triangle (rather than as a replacement) and if reserved for truly excellent sales performances (rather than overused and cheapened), recognition programs will motivate sales behavior. We have seen a mountain of evidence to this effect. We agree with sales consultant, Kent Stickler, who tells his workshop audiences that "money is good as long as it is accompanied by a pat on the back."

QUESTIONS SALESPEOPLE ASK

Salespeople frequently ask themselves several questions about the reward system in their institution (Futrell, 1981). One question is: *Are the rewards worth it?* "Is it worth it to me to make the extra effort to cross-sell or to make additional telephone calls to prospects?" It is in this context that the concept of the reward triangle becomes so important. Financial rewards or the possibility of career benefits or periodic recognition, standing alone, may not be enough to inspire superior efforts over time. Putting all three together, however, can be exceedingly powerful. The sample banks with the strongest sales reward systems use all three parts of the reward triangle.

A second question salespeople ask is: *What is the probability of success?* "Can I be a successful salesperson?" "Will hard work result in success?" Two ideas are relevant here. First, a number of the sample banks stressed positive rather than negative reinforcement to encourage personnel to want to sell rather than to force them to sell. One CEO stated: "Our system is designed to reward achievement, not to punish ineffectiveness." A senior executive from another bank said: "We don't believe in the whip." We concur with this approach. Preparing bankers for the sales role—and providing a positive, encouraging environment for them to test their skills and abilities—is more likely to result in a sustainable sales program than threats or coercion. Most people in work situations will try the new, asked-for behaviors if a "climate of trying" has been established.

Bankers will also be more optimistic about their own prospects as salespeople.if they are given the time to succeed. An evolutionary approach to building a sales program is recommended over a revolutionary approach, a point stressed in Chapter 4. As human resources expert, George Rieder, likes to put it in workshops on managing organizational change: "Fill the cup of change slowly."

Several sample banks developed their sales programs by purposely establishing low initial sales performance goals for salespeople. The goals were then raised as salespeople developed their skills and increased their confidence. One senior bank executive explained it this way:

> We don't want to set up the officer calling program for failure by setting our sights too high. We want the junior officers to experience success to show we are sincere in our commitment and to build their confidence. They have to want success. Then it's up to us to provide the tools and environment for success. Otherwise, we are setting them up for failure.

A third question is: *Will I be rewarded for my success?* "Will the promised rewards materialize if I do increase my selling efforts and productivity?" Making the connection between sales performance and rewards *definite* and *visible* is, we believe, the crucial concept in this regard. Although we subscribe to the "fill the cup slowly" theory, we do *not* agree with those who would avoid using the terms "selling" and "sales" in the bank. We think the words should be used—again and again—in performance appraisals, in house organ articles announcing job promotions, at banquets feting outstanding performers, and in other ways. The linkage between sales performance and rewards requires that the word "selling" be used.

CONCLUSION

Rewarding selling performance is an essential element in building a sales program. More than any of the other elements of the sales loop, a sales reward system gives selling behavior *credibility.* People know management is serious about selling if they get paid for it! The best sales reward systems incorporate direct financial rewards, career advancement, *and* recognition, rather than just one or even two of these elements. *The best reward systems cover all the bases!*

12

Developing
Selling Managers

"By working faithfully 8 hours a day, you may eventually get to be a boss and work 12 hours a day."

Robert Frost.

Special people—sales defenders, sales champions, sales managers—are the spark plugs of the bank's sales effort. They make it go. One such person is the often-called "forgotten hero" of the bank—the first-line sales manager. The person between the big boss and the individual salesperson.

First-line sales managers—having titles such as branch manager, CSR coordinator, sales coordinator, district manager, regional manager, or just sales manager—play a vitally important role in the effectiveness of a bank's sales program.

The importance of the salesperson's immediate superior was dramatically evident in a study made by a life insurance company (Davis, 1957). The company classified its branch managers—the immediate supervisors of sales personnel—into two categories: the half of the managers who were most effective and the half who were less effective.

The company then noted what happened to sales personnel who were recruited and trained at headquarters. Life insurance companies were among the first to develop accurate tests of sales abilities. Of sales recruits who rated "A" or "most effective" on screening tests, 48 percent became successful sales-

■ **The Sales Loop**

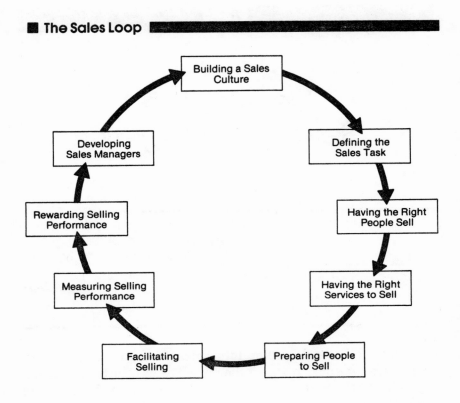

people under the best managers and only 27 percent under the less successful managers. Of sales recruits who rated "B" or lower, 27 percent succeeded under the best managers and only 6 percent under the poorer managers.

This study seems to indicate that persons of indifferent abilities are as likely to succeed under a good manager as are persons of outstanding abilities under a mediocre manager. Or, to put it another way, the quality of first-line supervision has as much to do with the sales staff's success as the drive and ability they bring to the job.

In bank after bank we saw similar evidence. One regional vice president talked about how he promoted his high-performing branch managers to larger and larger branches. He gave several examples of how he had promoted people to a larger branch that was performing below potential and within six-to-nine months a noticeable increase in performance and personnel morale occurred. Thus, we believe the sales culture and the leadership in the group, branch, or unit are critical to developing and maintaining an ongoing "all star" sales program.

THE SALES MANAGER'S JOB

The life and times of today's sales manager are challenging and often extremely demanding. The sales manager is given the responsibility of developing and/or maintaining an effective sales force. The manager is not so much a producer of sales as a producer of people who can produce sales.

Managing a sales force requires planning, organizing, staffing, directing, and controlling sales force activities, strategies, and tactics in order to generate sales that meet bank objectives. Sales managers work with and through individuals and groups in the bank, in the sales force, and outside of the bank to accomplish their goals.

The sales manager's main goal is to achieve the levels of sales volume, profits, and growth desired by higher levels of management. The factor underlying a manager's success in achieving this goal is the ability to influence the behavior of all parties involved. This includes the manager's ability to influence salespeople to do things that they would not do on their own.

The manager must be able to recruit good people and provide proper motivation and effective leadership. It is important to remember that sales managers are held responsible for the success of their salespeople. Consequently, sales managers are performance-oriented. They look for ways to make their salespeople more efficient and more effective.

Managerial Skills

It is generally felt that successful sales managers must have three types of skills: technical, human, and conceptual. These skills can be explained as:

- *Technical skill*: Ability to perform specific tasks, have great depth of knowledge of product, and be skilled in all phases of selling.

- *Human skill*: Ability to lead, build morale and effort, motivate, and manage conflict among subordinates.
- *Conceptual skill*: Ability to understand how one's own area of responsibility relates to the total operation of the organization. Also, ability to diagnose and assess management problems.

These skills are needed at all management levels, as shown in Figure 12–1 (Futrell, 1981). First-line managers need highly technical skills because they recruit and train salespeople and serve as role models. The higher the level, such as the person in charge of branch operations, the better a manager must be able to understand and relate sales management functions to the accomplishment of corporate goals. Human skills are equally important at each managerial level.

To be a successful sales manager, an individual must have excellent "human skills." John D. Rockefeller once stated: "I will pay more for the ability to deal with people than any other ability under the sun" (Bergen and Haney, 1966). Many feel that the most important skill of a manager—even more important than decisiveness, intelligence, job skills, or knowledge—is the ability to inspire and lead people. In fact, when bank salespeople were asked what the important qualifications for the sales

FIGURE 12-1 ■ Necessary Managerial Skills and Their Importance at Varying Management Levels ■■■■■■■■

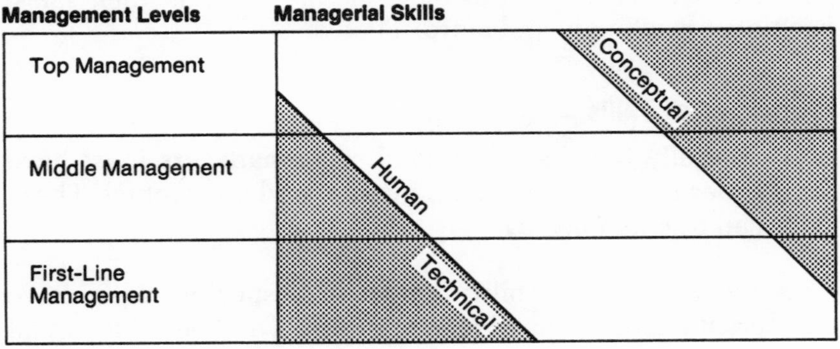

manager's job are, leadership was singled out as the most important.

SALES MANAGEMENT FUNCTIONS

This discussion of the sales manager's functions applies to each of the three basic levels of management. Whether the sales manager is in a top, middle, or first-line managerial position, five basic functions must be fulfilled, as indicated in Figure 12-2.

- *Planning:* Establishing a broad outline for goals, policies, and procedures that will result in accomplishing the objectives of the bank.
- *Organizing:* Setting up an administrative structure through which work activities are defined, subdivided, and coordinated to accomplish organizational goals.
- *Staffing:* Recruiting, hiring, and training.
- *Directing:* Dealing with people, positively and persuasively, from a leadership position.
- *Controlling:* Comparing actual performance to planned performance goals to determine whether to take corrective action if goals are not achieved or to continue using the same methods if goals were met.

FIGURE 12-2 ■ Sales Management Functions

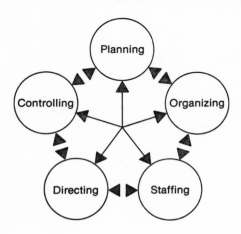

Time spent on each function. The amount of time that a sales manager spends performing each function depends on the manager's organizational level in the bank, as shown in Figure 12–3 (Futrell, 1981). First-line managers spend more time "directing" salespeople than higher level managers do. In comparison, top-level managers spend more time planning and organizing. This can be seen more clearly if we compare the job functions of the corporate sales executive to those of the first-line sales manager.

Corporate sales executive job functions.

- Planning—developing and implementing total bank sales goals, strategies, tactics, and policies.
- Organizing—developing the sales structure.
- Staffing—promoting and training sales managers.
- Directing—developing leadership and motivation strategies for the entire sales organization.
- Controlling—evaluating performance of total sales force.

FIGURE 12-3 ■ Relative Amount of Time Spent on Each Sales Management Function

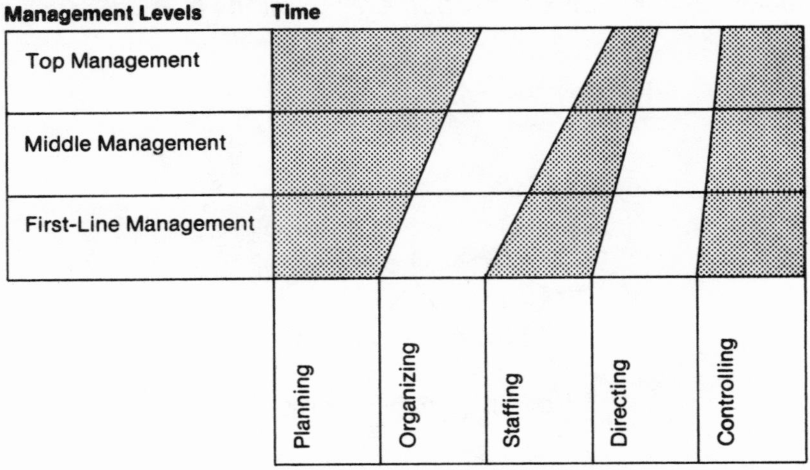

First-line sales manager job functions.

- Planning—developing and implementing specific objectives, strategies and tactics.
- Organizing—developing their sales group for effective customer service and/or account coverage.
- Staffing—recruiting, hiring, and training salespeople.
- Directing—leadership and motivation of their sales group.
- Controlling—evaluating individual and sales group performance.

IMPROVING THE SALES TEAM'S PERFORMANCE

What keeps a salesperson, group within the bank, or the bank itself from high performance? Chances are the reason involves the management of the sales team—maybe even one sales manager.

We found eight elements that are necessary to create an effective sales management function. These elements are also contained in the Sales Loop Model. They need to be only slightly changed and applied to the sales manager's job. The eight elements are:

1. Banks must have the right people to manage. Selection of sales managers is critical. Sales managers need to be both people-oriented and production-oriented. They need intelligence, energy, ego strength and drive, empathy, and other built-in capacities to succeed in a particular kind of sales management position within the bank.
2. Sales managers need the ability to hire the right people to sell. Some of this ability comes with training and experience. Some of it is "natural."
3. Sales managers need the ability to train salespeople. When salespeople are on the job, they turn to their sales manager for guidance. Thus, the manager should be knowledgeable in operations and sales, plus be a capable coach, mentor, and trainer.
4. Sales managers need reasonable support to train and field an all-star team. Money, facilities, personnel, sup-

plies, and encouragement are key resources needed by the sales manager. Sales management needs to be "facilitated" just as "selling" does.

5. Sales managers require clear standards of the performance that is expected of them and their salespeople. The sales management task must be defined, and top management needs to continually communicate their expectations of the sales force to their sales managers.

6. A system to measure the sales manager's performance needs to be developed and maintained over time. Goals must be set, and performance measured, evaluated, reported, and rewarded.

7. Sales managers need to be rewarded on their individual performance. To a large degree, this is based upon the group's performance.

8. Sales managers should have the opportunity to develop their skills and knowledge and to advance in the bank. Although first-line managers are decisive factors in the effectiveness of the sales force, their training and development is neglected in many banks. Salespeople go to sales training sessions, and top managers are sent to all kinds of management development courses, but the first-line manager is frequently forgotten. This should not happen.

We feel if only *one* of these elements is missing, average or below average sales performance is likely.

CONCLUSION

Sales managers play a vitally important role in the effectiveness of the bank's sales operation. They must plan, organize, staff, direct, and control sales force activities, strategies, and tactics in order to generate sales that meet bank objectives. The sales manager's main goal is to achieve the levels of sales volume, profits, and growth desired by higher levels of management.

Improving the sales team's performance requires the bank to:

1. Have the right people to manage.
2. Train the manager on how to hire winners.

3. Train the manager on how to train salespeople.
4. Facilitate sales management.
5. Define the sales manager's task.
6. Measure the sales manager's performance.
7. Reward the sales manager.
8. Allow for upward career movement for successful sales managers.

The sales manager is the "spark plug" of the bank's sales effort. Thus, the bank should do everything it can to help make this person successful. Give sales managers the resources and the praise they so richly deserve. To do so will pay big dividends.

Part Three

THE
CHALLENGE

13

Perspectives on Building a Sales Program

"I soon found out that the more people I talked to, the more sales I made."

Joe Girard, How to Sell Anything to Anybody, *Warner Books, 1977, p. 28.*

Personal selling is the future in bank marketing. Product lines have become too complex, banks' relationship-building objectives have become too important, and competitors both inside and outside of banking have become too aggressive for non-personal communications and order-taking to be sufficient. Bankers *must* sell in the newly deregulated, intensely competitive financial services business.

But will they sell? Is it possible to turn traditionally un-aggressive banking institutions that prospered in yesterday's highly structured, rate-protected marketplace into lean and hungry sales organizations? Can it be done? Is it a realistic objective? If so, where do you start? What are the essential elements of a strong program? How do you keep the program going? Keep the momentum after the newness wears off?

This book represents the culmination of a multi-year, multi-part research effort to answer these questions. We conducted the research because we believed personal selling to be absolutely critical to a bank's marketing success in today's and tomorrow's marketplace. Yet we sensed that most banks either were struggling to make the transition to a more selling-aggressive posture or had not yet recognized the imperative of selling and essentially were doing nothing to develop a sales program.

We have learned from our research that bankers can and will sell. We have learned that it is possible for a bank to become a lean and hungry sales organization. We have learned that it *can be done.* We have also learned that it is tough to do. Building a strong, sustainable sales program is an imposing, elusive, difficult challenge. It cannot be done overnight. "Crash" programs are not the answer. Magical or easy solutions do not exist. And an effective sales program will not happen unless top management is deeply committed to having it and knows what to do to achieve this state.

THE SALES LOOP MODEL

The central conclusion of this book is the existence of *sales program success factors.* The same factors influence the successful sales programs we studied. It does not matter if the program is directed to the retail market or the wholesale market. It does not matter if the bank is large or small. It does not matter if the bank is a unit bank or a branching bank. The steps in building and maintaining a strong sales program are *universal.* We have incorporated these success factors in the Sales Loop Model, which is shown again in Figure 13-1.

The Sales Loop Model is a "blueprint" for developing a new sales program or improving an existing one. For new programs, it presents a sequence of "task areas." For example, the qualities sought when hiring new salespeople should be influenced by the specific selling roles they will be expected to perform. Sales personnel should have formal preparation for the selling role before being measured in this role. And so on through the loop. There is a rationale for the ordering in which the loop model elements are presented that should be helpful to bank executives just starting out to build a sales program.

The Sales Loop Model contributes in a different way to bank executives attempting to improve an existing sales program rather than to start a new one. The underlying premise of the Sales Loop Model is that nine key elements must be present for a bank to fully realize its potential as a selling institution. Weakness in just one of these elements will impede realization

FIGURE 13-1 ■ The Sales Loop ▬▬▬▬▬▬▬▬▬▬

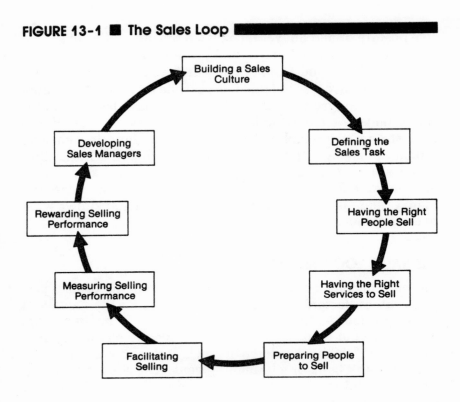

of this potential. Accordingly, improvement of an existing sales program would revolve around an honest and careful assessment of the program, the identification of the sales loop elements in which the bank is weak, and the development of a step-by-step action plan for overcoming these weaknesses.

Having studied banks that are strong with all nine elements and banks that are strong with just six or seven, we are prepared to state, as clearly, as powerfully, as emphatically as we can, that a first-rate sales program requires strength in *all* nine areas. A bank needs to close the sales loop and keep it closed!

The Sales Loop Model, then, is a blueprint for action. But it is a broad blueprint, not a detailed one. The blueprint is actionable to the degree that the model's fundamental concepts, nuances, intricacies, and interrelationships are understood. It is actionable to the degree that one understands that each of the loop model elements requires continuing attention and investment. The Sales Loop Model can seem intoxicatingly simple if one merely looks at it and doesn't take the time to read and think through the supporting detail in the chapters that describe each element. Implementing the sales loop model is anything but simple.

SUMMING UP

We close this book with some of the perspectives we are left with based on the research, thinking, and reading we have done over the past several years on selling in banking. The ideas that follow have been presented in one form or another earlier in the book. We hope that pulling them together in summary fashion will re-emphasize their importance.

1. The banks with the strongest sales programs are exceedingly well-managed banks overall. They are high-performing banks, not just high-performing selling banks. The qualities that contribute to sound bank management are not materially different from those necessary to build a sales program.

2. The nature, strength, and continuity of a bank's dominant values are central to its ability to build an effective, sustainable sales program. Banks that are genuinely customer-oriented, that take a missionary zeal to providing high-quality services, that seek to be "easy to do business with"—these banks have a big "head start" over others in developing a first-rate sales program. The longer these values have been in place, the better.

3. Building a sales program requires taking the long view. The "quick fix" temptation must be avoided at all costs. The sense of urgency to pull a sales program together is very real in many banks. To be sure, there is no time to waste. Yet, cosmetic or simplistic efforts will surely fail. What is needed is a plan for installing (or rebuilding) a sales program that can be implemented in stages. The mind-set should be "evolution" rather than "revolution."

4. The sales defender and sales champion functions required to nurture a sales culture should be firmly in place from the very beginning of a sales program's development. The sales defender role is necessary to protect the process by which a program is implemented from naysayers, budget cutters, and others. The sales champion role is necessary to conceive, co-ordinate, steer, and rally the process itself. Good intentions are not enough. The sales defender and champion roles must be performed.

5. The most effective sales programs have "sales teams," not just "salespeople." We found much evidence in our research of salespeople working together, sharing information, thinking in terms of group sales goals in addition to individual goals, and feeling as though they were part of something rather than alone. Most people enjoy the sense of "team," the sense of striving and accomplishing together. Moreover, the presence and support of a group is one of the primary ways people can adjust to significant change in their lives, such as being asked to be a salesperson, when they never before have been. Every advantage should be taken of team-building approaches available.

6. Senior managers must set a *sales example*. Assisting on important sales calls, making sales calls themselves, presiding over sales meetings, being willing to pay for sales—in these and other ways top management can demonstrate its commitment to the sales program. People in organizations have an uncanny knack for figuring out management's *true* priorities. Management only casually committed to a sales program will not be successful faking full commitment.

7. Salesperson motivation depends on a strong linkage among specific sales tasks, sales goals, sales measurement, and sales rewards. Salespeople *need to know:* (1) what it is they are supposed to do; (2) the goals they are striving for; (3) how they are doing; and (4) that they will be rewarded if they do what they are supposed to do.

8. Input shapes output. Staffing the sales force with people who are empathetic, assertive, motivated, interpersonally skillful, and have the other attributes enumerated in Chapter 6 leads to better results than if the sales force is staffed differently. The banks with the best sales programs take great care in hiring and assigning personnel for customer-contact positions. Staffing sales positions is viewed as a "high-stakes" endeavor. Few decisions are seen as more important.

9. Bank salespeople need to understand and believe in the services they are asked to sell. Knowledge of services breeds salesperson confidence. So does the innovativeness and quality of services. And *confidence breeds motivation.* Bankers who can knowledgeably discuss a service's features and benefits with a prospect—and who genuinely believe that the service is outstanding—will be more motivated to sell it than if they lack confidence either in the service or in their own knowledge of it.

10. The mandate to "train the salesforce"—which is crucial—does not go far enough. Salespeople require sales skills training, to be sure. But they also require sales-related knowledge—knowledge of services, knowledge of the sales role, knowledge of the customer, knowledge of the environment in which the bank competes. Preparing people to sell involves *combining* education and training; it involves sales knowledge development *and* sales skills development.

11. Sales skills development needs to extend beyond the classroom. People develop sales skills by "doing," not by just "listening." Live, "hands-on" selling experiences coupled with the feedback of coaches or mentors, practice sessions, videotaped role-playing sessions—these are the stuff of effective sales skills development.

12. The banks with the strongest sales programs have encouraged their salespeople to develop their own selling styles. These banks provide input concerning selling approaches and techniques, but then they allow salespeople to use this input as they see fit. These banks see no need to turn out "cookie cutter" salespeople. Managerial dictates are held to an effective minimum. The emphasis is on results rather than on procedures.

13. The most effective bank marketing departments are not those that are exceptionally clever in practicing marketing; rather, they are those that are exceptionally clever in getting everyone else in the bank to practice marketing. These marketing departments devote considerable time, energy, and resources to making it easier for bank employees to sell the bank's services.

14. Measuring sales performance is essential. A bank will not come close to realizing its potential as a selling organization if it does not keep score. Personnel asked to sell need to know that others will know how they are doing. The most effective sales measurement systems report names next to results, are timely, accurate, easy to understand and fair, emphasize results rather than efforts, and contribute to sales task clarity by focusing on the key selling behaviors expected.

15. Few actions have a more telling impact on an organization's culture than the behaviors that get rewarded. A sales program must have *teeth* to be perceived as legitimate. Bank managements seeking to build strong sales cultures must be prepared to reward selling behavior in three ways: direct financial rewards, career advancement, and recognition. The *link* between sales performance and rewards must be clearcut, strong, and visible. Doubt should not exist in the organization concerning whether selling performance "pays off."

16. For a great many bank salespeople, the psychology of rewards means as much or more to motivating sales behavior than the rewards themselves. How management rewards sales performance can be as critical or even more critical than "how much" the rewards involve. We have seen firsthand in our research the strong motivational impact of a CEO personally congratulating a calling officer on a big sale. We have seen firsthand the strong impact of a commission system that pays customer service representatives only $50 or $75 a month in extra compensation. We have seen firsthand the impact of "peer pressure," perhaps the most powerful motivator of them all. What rewards *mean to people* counts.

17. Each of the Sales Loop Model elements applying to salespeople also applies to their supervisors, who are sales managers. Reaching the supervisor with the sales message, defining the sales management task, preparing supervisors for sales management responsibilities, tying their rewards to the sales success of subordinates—it is only in these and other ways that the sales loop can actually be closed. The sales loop will remain open—and the sales program will be of limited effectiveness—until the *people that salespeople work for* emphasize selling behavior in the day-to-day process of managing.

18. The sales group in any bank can be divided into three categories: high performers, average performers, and poor performers. A key challenge in improving a bank's selling effectiveness is materially upgrading the production of average performers. Another key is making the poor performing group smaller. The need to properly reward high performers should not draw managerial attention away from the opportunities for moving average producers up a notch or two and for, one way or the other, reducing the size of the low producing group.

19. Salespeople need to have the time to sell. It is difficult for customer service representatives to cross-sell bank services with one customer when three other customers are sitting nearby waiting to open an account. It is difficult for calling officers to make calls when mountains of paperwork cover their desks. Eliminating unnecessary non-selling duties from a salesperson's job, investing in technology that simplifies the booking of business, assuring that sales desks are adequately covered during peak times—these actions are part and parcel of building a sales program.

ONE FINAL THOUGHT

Building an effective sales program is a complex, multi-faceted challenge. It is not an easy thing to do. Being interested in having a sales program is a far cry from having a sales program. We sense that at least some of the time what appears to be top management resistance to investing in a sales program is in fact not resistance. The problem is that top management doesn't really know what to do to build a sales program and they are not confident that the proposals coming from the marketing department for a training program, or for a commission sales system, or for something else, will get the job done. And they are right. A sales training program or a commission sales system, standing alone, will not be enough. Developing an effective sales program requires that all of the pieces of the puzzle fit together. Developing an effective sales program requires that it indeed be a *program*. It is this overriding idea that we hope we have communicated with the word-picture of the Sales Loop Model.

REFERENCES

Chapter 1

Donnelly, James H., and Leonard L. Berry. (1981) "Bank Marketing: Past, Present, Future." In James H. Donnelly and William R. George, eds., *Marketing of Services*. Chicago: American Marketing Association, pp. 66–70.

Kendall, Richard L. (1984) "What's Missing in Officer Call Programs That Fail." *Bank Marketing*, January, p. 14.

(1983) "The Science of Selling," *The Royal Bank Letter*, The Royal Bank of Canada, November–December.

Chapter 2

Futrell, Charles M. (1981) *Sales Management: Behavior, Practices, and Cases*. Hinsdale, Ill.: Dryden Press, pp. 248–250.

Stickler, Kent. (1982) "Personal Selling in Retail Banking." *Journal of Retail Banking*, June, pp. 74–82.

Chapter 4

Biggart, Nicole Woolsey. (1977) "The Creative-Destructive Process of Organizational Change: The Case of the Post Office." *Administrative Science Quarterly*, September, pp. 410-426.

Deal, Terrence E., and Allan A. Kennedy. (1982) *Corporate Cultures—The Rites and Rituals of Corporate Life*. Reading, Mass.: Addison-Wesley Publishing.

Peters, Thomas J. (1978) "Symbols, Patterns, and Settings: An Optimistic Case for Getting Things Done." *Organizational Dynamics*, Autumn, pp. 3–22.

Silverzweig, Stan, and Robert F. Allen. (1976) "Changing the Corporate Culture." *Sloan Management Review*, Spring, pp. 33–49.

Chapter 5

Churchill, Gilbert A., Jr., Neil M. Ford, and Orville C. Walker, Jr. (1976) "Organizational Climate and Job Satisfaction in the Salesforce." *Journal of Marketing Research,* November, pp. 323–332.

Doyle, Stephen X., and Benson P. Shapiro. (1980) "What Counts Most in Motivating Your Sales Force." *Harvard Business Review,* May–June, pp. 133–140.

Futrell, Charles M., John E. Swan, and John T. Todd. (1976) "Job Performance Related to Management Control Systems for Pharmaceutical Salesmen." *Journal of Marketing Research,* February, pp. 25–33.

Shapiro, Benson P., and Stephen X. Doyle. (1983) "Make the Sales Task Clear." *Harvard Business Review,* November–December, pp. 72, 76.

Chapter 6

Ford, Neil M., and Orville C. Walker, Jr. (1984) "Sales Management Research: State of the Art and Future Needs." Paper presented at the fourth annual American Marketing Association Faculty Consortium.

Futrell, Charles M. (1981) *Sales Management: Behavior, Practice, and Cases.* Hinsdale, Ill.: Dryden Press.

Ivancevich, John M., and William F. Glueck. (1983) *Foundations of Personnel: Human Resource Management.* Plano, Tex.: Business Publications.

Ivancevich, John M., James H. Donnelly, Jr., and James L. Gibson. (1983) *Managing for Performance.* Plano, Tex.: Business Publications.

Stewart, Charles J., and William B. Cash, Jr. (1982) *Interviewing: Principles and Practices.* Dubuque, Iowa: William C. Brown.

Chapter 7

Stanton, William J. (1984) *Fundamentals of Marketing.* New York: McGraw-Hill, pp. 179–181.

Townsend, Robert C. (1970) *Up the Organization.* New York: Alfred A. Knopf.

Futrell, Charles. (1981) *Sales Management: Behavior, Practice and Cases.* Hinsdale, Ill.: Dryden Press.

Chapter 8

De Marco, William M., and Michael D. Maginn. (1982) *Sales Competency Research Report.* Forum Corporation.

Negri, Robert. (1973) "A Sales Training Program for Affiliates." *Bank Marketing,* December, pp. 25–28.

Rieder, George. (1982) "Nobody Will Buy If You Don't Ask Them—Building a Professional Sales Force." Bank Marketing Association National Convention, Phoenix, Arizona, October 25.

Chapter 9

Barger, Steven B. (1984) "The Investor Center: A 'Special' Delivery System that Hawkeye Built." *Bank Marketing,* March, pp. 16–18.

Drucker, Peter F. (1973–74) *Management: Tasks, Responsibilities, Practices.* New York: Harper & Row Publishers, p. 519.

Futrell, Charles. (1984) *Fundamentals of Selling.* Homewood, Ill.: Richard D. Irwin.

Chapter 10

Berry, Alexander, B., and Lawrence A. Williams. (1984) "Commercial Selling According to Plan." *Bank Marketing,* March, pp. 31–33.

Futrell, Charles. (1984) *Fundamentals of Selling,* Homewood, Ill.: Richard D. Irwin.

Chapter 11

Bennett, Andrea. (1984) "Incentive Programs Gaining Popularity among Bankers." *American Banker,* April 3, pp. 31–32.

Futrell, Charles. (1981) *Sales Management: Behavior, Practice, and Cases.* Hinsdale, Ill.: Dryden Press.

Walker, Orville C., Gilbert A. Churchill, and Neil M. Ford. (1977) "Motivation and Performance in Industrial Selling: Present

Knowledge and Needed Research." *Journal of Marketing Research*, May, pp. 156–168.

Herzberg, Frederick, B. Mausner, and B. Snyderman. (1959) *The Motivation To Work*, 2d ed. New York: John Wiley & Sons.

Lawler, Edwin E. (1971) *Pay and Organizational Effectiveness: A Psychological View*. New York: McGraw-Hill.

Chapter 12

Bergen, Garret L., and William V. Haney. (1966) *Organizational Relations and Management*. New York: McGraw-Hill. p. 3.

Davis, Robert T. (1957) *Performance and Development of Field Sales Managers*. Boston: Division of Research, Harvard University Graduate School of Business Administration, p. 65.

Futrell, Charles. (1981) *Sales Management: Behavior, Cases, and Practices*. Hinsdale, Ill.: Dryden Press.

Index